EASY 30-MINUTE STIR·FRY COOKBOOK

[EASY] 30-MINUTE STIR·FRY COOKBOOK

90 Asian Recipes for Your Wok or Skillet

Chris Toy

Photography by Iain Bagwell

ROCKRIDGE PRESS

To Alex, Cameron, and Lindsay. So many fond memories in the kitchen and around the dinner table. Be sure to eat your vegetables!
Love you, Dad

CONTENTS

INTRODUCTION

Some of my earliest memories of family life are connected to the pleasant sensations of stir-frying. As children, my sister and I were required to nap after we returned home from elementary school while our mom prepared dinner. We would wake up to the sounds of sizzling meat and the pungent scent of ginger, garlic, and scallions. The click-click-click of Mom's metal spatula against her wok beckoned us to the kitchen.

I can still see us all gathered around the dinner table. In front of Dad, a steaming bowl of rice. Another serving bowl filled with stir-fried meat, onions, carrots, peppers, and bok choy, seasoned with ginger, garlic, and soy sauce. Dad would smile and chuckle under his breath after saying grace as he anticipated the day's reward, just before reaching for the rice to serve us. During dinner, we shared the day's stories and news of the family and neighborhood. Of course, we cleaned our plates, and I usually asked for—and got—seconds. Mom always made extra rice to make fried rice the next day, which never lasted long enough to go into the refrigerator.

Variations of this memory occurred on a larger scale at family gatherings. Birthdays, holidays, anniversaries, and visits from out-of-town guests were all reasons to come together for bowls of rice or noodles and stir-fry. One great thing about these gatherings was the variety of dishes; each family would contribute their own specialty. This tradition of sharing also extended to church suppers. Many of Mom's and my aunties' recipes found their way into the church recipe books.

Both my parents' families owned Chinese restaurants. My dad's family owned Toy's Chinese Restaurant in Milwaukee, Wisconsin, for over 80 years. Mom's family opened King Joy, the first Chinese restaurant in Quincy, Massachusetts, in the 1930s. Our extended family owned and worked in restaurants in San Francisco, Chicago, New York, and Boston. Whenever and wherever I have gathered with family and friends, the sights, sounds, aromas, and flavors of good stir-fry were always present.

This tradition of gathering to share stir-fry and companionship has always been a significant aspect of my life that continues today. Whether it was making a quick, inexpensive meal in a studio apartment over an electric hot plate in college, bringing colleagues together for a Chinese New Year celebration, enjoying a weekend dinner with friends, or sharing tips and techniques with students in a cooking class, I have been recreating those early, delightful stir-fry memories throughout my life.

My wish in writing this cookbook is that through learning stir-fry, you will enjoy these meals with your family and friends as you exchange stories, chuckle together, and savor the fruits of your labor. You'll see how quick, easy, and delicious creating tasty stir-fry at home can be. Perhaps you'll even venture beyond these recipes and create your own signature meals! With a sturdy wok and a curious mind, you'll be making your own memories in no time.

[ONE]

STIR-FRY IN A FLASH

Stir-fry cooking literally describes itself. It's as easy as 1-2-3: tools, preparation, and technique. The recipes, steps, and tips in this book will teach you how to deliver a delicious, successful stir-fry every time—no soggy veggies or rubbery meat. With a handful of the right tools, some preparation, and a little practice, you will be stir-frying delicious meals in no time.

In this chapter, we'll go over what tools you'll need to create great stir-fry dishes. I'll explain the trade-offs among different tools, as well as teach you how to care for them, especially your wok or skillet and your knife. Finally, you'll learn some basic principles of stir-frying, a short history of where it came from, and an exploration of how it has expanded globally from its origins in China.

Faster Than Takeout

Stir-fry is the original quick, one-pot meal. Just heat some oil, stir in your sliced ingredients for a few minutes, add sauce, and dinner is served! In the time it takes for you to place your takeout order, pick it up at the restaurant, and come back home, you can whip up your own super-fresh, cheap, and tasty stir-fry.

Cleanup is also a breeze. Just rinse and wipe down your well-seasoned wok or skillet with some hot water. Dry it well and put it away (or, if you're like me, leave it on your cooktop ready for your next meal!).

Stir-fry is my go-to menu item when entertaining at home, as I can prepare most of the ingredients in advance. Or dinner prep can be part of the party! It also makes it easy to accommodate dietary preferences—just cook a different mix of ingredients in two or more batches. Lastly, you know what's going into your food, so you can avoid things like too much sugar, salt, or gluten. And if you really like something, you can always toss in some extra—think bonus scallops, tofu, or snow peas. The world's your oyster (or shrimp or lobster)!

A Quick History

Stir-fry typically refers to the process of quickly cooking tender, juicy, chopstick-size (or bite-size) ingredients with aromatics such as ginger or garlic in hot oil. A savory sauce and raw garnish, such as scallions, chives, or other fresh herbs, are often added just as the heat is turned off. Fast and no frills, stir-frying makes efficient use of time, energy, and resources.

Archaeological evidence indicates that Chinese cooks were stir-frying in woks more than 2,000 years ago. Over centuries, the stir-fry technique spread from its Chinese origins to other parts of Asia and beyond. Chinese-style stir-fry both influenced and was influenced by the cultures it encountered as the practice spread globally.

Within Asia, stir-fry cooking takes many different forms. Japanese stir-fry has soy sauce in common with Chinese stir-fry but does not include the heavier, more pungent flavors such as hot sesame oil and oyster sauce. Teriyaki, a light, sweet sauce, is unique to Japanese stir-fry. Thailand and Vietnam also have notable differences and similarities in their stir-fry recipes, both favoring the more delicate rice noodles and fragrant jasmine rice. Thai stir-fry is influenced by Indian flavors, using hot curries and peppers, while

Vietnamese stir-fry includes lighter-flavored fish sauce, more fresh herbs, and less spice. Indian, Myanmarese, and Malaysian stir-fry use shredded or finely chopped coconut or coconut milk and are traditionally spicy.

When Chinese immigrants arrived in America in the 1800s, prospecting gold, working on the railroads, or seeking fortunes, they brought with them woks and the method of stir-frying, and created what are now Chinese-American restaurants. They adapted traditional Chinese recipes with available ingredients and preferred tastes in the United States. Popular Chinese-American stir-fry dishes, such as the sweet General Tso's Chicken created in the 1970s, taste very different from the original 1950s hot and sour Taiwanese versions.

Essential Equipment

One of the many benefits of stir-frying is that it requires relatively little kitchen equipment to make a satisfying meal. In this section, I will describe the equipment necessary for creating these dishes, detail the benefits of specific tools, and provide some cultural and historical information about them. By the end of this section, you will know exactly what equipment you will need to make the most delicious stir-fry, as well as possess the information necessary to make any informed equipment purchases, should you choose to do so.

▸ Woks

The word "wok" simply means "pan" in Cantonese. In the Mandarin dialect, a wok is referred to as a kuo. Woks were developed around 2,000 years ago and are still the most ideal vessels for stir-frying today. The wok's small, rounded bottom makes efficient use of limited fuel by concentrating heat and then distributing it evenly along the curved surface, eliminating hot spots that may cause food to stick and burn. The curve also allows the oil and ingredients to move to the wok's hottest part. This creates the stir-fry's signature high sizzle, quickly searing in flavor and juice and imparting a subtle smoky flavor known as wok hei, which metaphorically translates to "breath of the wok."

Woks are traditionally made by hammering a disk of carbon steel into a bowl shape and attaching one or two handles. Wok-like pans are used throughout Asia, and different cultures have customized the versatile pan to fit their needs. For example, the Cantonese wok, also known as a "two-eared wok," has two small, curved handles on each side. A Northern-style wok usually has one long removable wooden handle, sometimes with a handle on the opposite side for lifting when the wok is full. The Japanese refer to their wok-shaped pans as chukanabe, while in Southern India, their wok-shaped pans are referred to as cheena chatti. Both translate roughly to "Chinese pot."

Nowadays, woks come in many different shapes, sizes, and materials. When it comes to shape, woks are typically either round-bottomed or flat-bottomed. Round-bottomed woks were designed to be used over an open flame, so they are best suited for a gas stovetop. If you have a round-bottomed wok but an electric stove, place the wok ring that comes with the pan with the wider edge facing up to cradle the wok closest to the heat source. It might take a little more time for the wok to heat up since the heat is indirect, but once hot, the electric burner should be able to maintain adequate stir-frying temperature. In contrast, flat-bottomed woks were developed to accommodate electric flat-topped burners. If using a flat-bottomed wok, you may need to use a little more oil to compensate for hot spots that naturally occur. Hot spots are parts of the pan where the seasoning is beginning to burn; swirl the oil over those areas before adding any ingredients to prevent the food from burning.

The size of the wok you choose should be based on the maximum number of people you'll be cooking for. Nine-inch woks work well for one to two people, while 12-inch woks are better for two to four diners. Most family-size woks are 14 inches across and can prepare stir-fry for four to six people. Note that because of the wok's curved shape, it is possible to prepare stir-fry for just a few people in a large wok. But if the wok is too small, it will be challenging to stir-fry for a larger group without resorting to cooking in batches.

Regarding materials, I recommend using a cast-iron wok, as it is the most versatile and can maintain the high temperature necessary for searing and imparting wok hei. It can withstand heat from various fuel sources, including propane, wood, and charcoal. Cast iron is magnetic, so it also works on induction stovetops. A carbon steel wok is also a good choice, as it is easily seasoned and lighter than cast iron, making it easier to handle.

Finally, if you have an electric wok and have no other way to cook on your stovetop, it is possible to approximate stir-frying. However, using an electric wok has its drawbacks; they often cannot maintain the high temperature necessary for stir-frying, are usually coated with fragile materials that break down under high heat, and cannot be seasoned like carbon steel and cast iron.

SEASONING AND CARING FOR YOUR WOK

If you take care of your wok, it can last you a lifetime. Here's everything you need to know about seasoning and caring for your wok, so you can make memories with it for years to come!

Seasoning a new wok

1. Scrub your wok thoroughly with soap and hot water to remove any protective oil. Let dry.

2. If possible, remove the wooden handles. If that's not possible, soak paper towels in water and wrap the handles, then wrap the wet towels in a double layer of aluminum foil.

3. Soak a paper towel with vegetable, peanut, or avocado oil. I recommend avocado oil, as it has the highest smoke point and stands up well to the high temperatures required for stir-frying.

4. With the oiled paper towel, wipe the inside and outside of the wok without leaving any excess.

5. Place the wok upside down on a baking sheet and bake in the oven at 400°F for 15 minutes. Remove and let cool.

6. Repeat steps 4 and 5 two or three more times for a durable coating. Check the wooden parts to see if the water has evaporated and rewet the paper towels if needed.

CONTINUED >

Seasoning an old, rusty wok

1. Use a metal scrubbing pad and abrasive powder to remove the rust. Rinse thoroughly. Proceed from step 2 as if seasoning a new wok.

Caring for your wok

1. Rinse it out with just hot water—no soap!—and rub with a cloth to remove food particles.

2. Remove stuck-on food with a non-scratch sponge.

3. Wipe the wok dry, then place it on a baking sheet upside down and bake on medium heat for 5 minutes.

4. If you are not going to use the wok for a week or more, wipe the inside lightly with oil before storing it.

Tips for maintaining your wok's seasoning

1. Do not boil, poach, or steam in your newly seasoned wok.

2. Do not cook acidic foods like tomatoes, lemon, and vinegar in a newly seasoned wok.

3. Each time you stir-fry, the more nonstick it will become.

▸ Skillets

No wok? No worries! If you have a heavy skillet, you can still make stir-fry. Cast iron, carbon steel, and stainless steel are the best materials to use. Cast-iron skillets heat very evenly at high temperatures and are easily seasoned, making them good at searing ingredients in a stir-fry. Carbon steel skillets heat faster, are lighter, and will season well, but they will develop hot spots unless the bottom is thick and heavy. Good-quality stainless steel will heat evenly and can, over time, be seasoned to a degree. Note that a skillet, with its shallower sides, will not hold as much stir-fry as a wok of the same diameter; for that reason, I recommend using a 12-inch or larger skillet. Also note that a skillet will not heat as evenly as a wok, so you won't be able to get it as hot without some burning and sticking. In order to compensate, you will need to use a little more oil than you would in a wok. I highly recommend stir-frying with avocado oil, as it can handle temperatures over 500°F before breaking down and burning. The recipes in this book are designed for a wok, so if you are using a skillet to stir-fry, add an extra teaspoon of oil for every tablespoon indicated in the recipe.

▸ Other Tools

The essential list of kitchen tools you will need to successfully stir-fry is very short. Here's what I use daily:

Chinese all-purpose cleaver. Since stir-frying depends on quickly cooking bite-size pieces of food, you will need a sharp knife. I recommend an all-purpose Chinese cleaver. Its wide blade surface is easy to guide and control, and it can also be used to flatten and smash ingredients, such as garlic and ginger. The back of the blade and the handle's butt can even be used to tenderize meat and grind spices.

Cutting boards. Two or three boards large enough to keep all your ingredients on the board while prepping will be fine. Use one board for vegetables and the other for meat and fish. Wood and plastic are preferred; ceramic and glass will dull the edge of your knife.

Prep bowls. With all the slicing and chopping, you'll want a variety of bowls for organizing the prepared ingredients that are going into the hot wok. Three to four different-size bowls should be sufficient for a typical stir-fry.

Large stirring spoon or curved spatula. I use a long-handled metal stirring spoon for stir-frying. Its curved shape works well with the rounded wok surface. The spoon can also mix and serve glazes and gravies to accompany your stir-fry dishes. The traditional curved wok spatula also works well. A well-seasoned wok can withstand the brisk stirring of metal utensils, but if you have a wok or skillet with a nonstick surface, you will need to use high-temperature silicon or wooden utensils.

Soup ladle. Though not strictly used for stir-frying, a ladle is useful for serving tasty soups that begin with stir-fried ingredients.

Now that you have your tools, know how to care for them, and have a little history under your belt, you're almost ready for stir-fry mastery. On to essential ingredients to stock your stir-fry kitchen, and helpful tips to perfect your stir-fry technique.

CARING FOR YOUR KNIFE/CLEAVER:

It is impossible to stir-fry without a way to slice, chop, mince, or crush ingredients before cooking them. Whether you use a chef's knife or an all-purpose Chinese cleaver, it is important to maintain a sharp blade. It is said that a sharp knife will cut where you direct it. A dull knife will slip and cut you. Here are four basic rules for taking care of your knives.

1. Keep your cleaver or knife sharp by honing it with a steel before and after using it. If you do this each time you use it, the edge should remain keen.

2. Always use wooden or plastic cutting boards. A glass or metal cutting surface will ruin your edge, requiring sharpening beyond honing.

3. Never place cleavers or knives in the dishwasher. The action of the water and food particles against the edge during the wash cycle is like using your knife thousands of times without honing it.

4. Always store your cleaver or knife in its own holder, protecting the edge. Do not toss it in a drawer with other kitchen tools. Store it in a block holder or plastic scabbard, wrap it in cloth or leather, or attach it to a magnetic strip in your kitchen.

Malaysian Chicken [page 85]

THE EASY, 30-MINUTE STIR-FRY KITCHEN

If 30 minutes to prepare a tasty stir-fry dish sounds super-fast, that's because it is! Great stir-fry takes preparation and practice, but once you've got the basics down, 30-minute stir-fry success is completely possible. To get started, gather all the tools and equipment you'll be using from beginning to end and organize them for easy access. Next, prepare all your ingredients and arrange them in the order they will be used. If you want starch with your stir-fry, you'll need to start steaming your rice or boiling water for your noodles before firing up your wok, since they will take longer to cook than your stir-fry ingredients. When you're ready to serve, your guests will be impressed with the results and with how easy you made it all look!

Pantry Staples

In order to make the best stir-fry, you will need to stock your pantry with a few key ingredients. Below is my list of the necessities, along with quick tips on how to use them.

Chinese Rice Wine (Shaoxing brand recommended)

Chinese cooking wine is a dry rice wine for marinating and tenderizing meat. It is often used for glazes along with cornstarch and soy sauce.

QUICK TIP: If you don't have rice wine, you can use dry sherry or gin.

Cornstarch

The finely milled germ of corn kernels is called cornstarch. It is often whisked into liquids to thicken sauces and glazes during stir-frying, or used to coat ingredients for shallow and deep frying.

QUICK TIP: You can use a 50/50 mixture of regular flour and cornstarch to coat ingredients for deep-frying. Cornstarch crisps up before browning, while flour gives the fry a nice, chewy texture.

Fish Sauce

This highly pungent sauce is used in small amounts to add a strong umami flavor to many Asian stir-fry dishes, and needs no refrigeration. It is made from salted fish or shrimp that has been fermented for two to three years.

QUICK TIP: You do not want to spill fish sauce on anything porous.

Five-Spice Powder

Although there may be more than five spices in five-spice powder, five particular kinds are always present: star anise, Sichuan peppercorns, fennel, cloves, and cinnamon. Other spices added may include cloves, ginger, licorice, cardamom, or orange peel.

QUICK TIP: Dry roast equal parts table salt and five-spice powder to create a handy seasoning salt.

Garlic

A common aromatic in stir-fry, garlic is one of three key components in the Chinese flavor base, along with ginger and scallions. In addition to great flavor, garlic is considered to have many health benefits. If you grow garlic in your garden, the green parts can also be used in a stir-fry.

QUICK TIP: Keep a jar of pre-minced garlic in the fridge for when you're short on time; otherwise, store your garlic bulbs in a dark, dry place. You can also pickle garlic for longer-term storage.

Mirin (Japanese rice wine)

Mirin is a sweet Japanese cooking wine. It is used near the end of the cooking process to remove strong fishy flavors in a stir-fry.

QUICK TIP: You can substitute a sweet white wine such as sherry, moscato, ice wine, or dessert wine for mirin.

Rice Vinegars

Asian rice vinegars come from China, Japan, Korea, Thailand, and Vietnam. They range from light amber to red, brown, and even black. The darker vinegars have stronger flavor. Japanese and Korean vinegars are light and mild, while dark Chinese toasted rice vinegar has a stronger flavor. Vietnamese vinegars can be spicy, hot, and sour.

QUICK TIP: Western vinegars, such as balsamic and apple cider, tend to have stronger flavors. If substituted for rice vinegars, the quantity should be cut in half.

Stir-Fry Oil

A requirement for stir-frying, oil must withstand high temperatures to quickly sear meat and vegetables without breaking down. Burnt oil forms harmful carcinogens and ruins flavor. The best oil for stir-frying is avocado oil. It has a neutral flavor and the highest smoking point of any oil at 550°F. Other oils that withstand stir-fry temperatures are peanut, soybean, safflower, canola, coconut, and sunflower.

QUICK TIP: Do not mix a low-temperature oil with a high-temperature oil. Mixing does not "average out" the smoking point. The low-temperature oil will burn at its low smoking point, and the high-temperature oil will not reach stir-frying temperature.

Soy Sauce

Soy sauce is made by fermenting soybeans with a fungus, called aspergillus, and wheat in a salty brine for two to three years. Soy sauce that is labeled gluten-free has been brewed without wheat.

QUICK TIP: Soy sauce is salty enough that it does not need to be refrigerated.

Tamari

Tamari is a Japanese soy sauce and a byproduct of fermenting soybeans for miso. Rice is usually used in making tamari. However, some miso is fermented with other grains, so if you are gluten-free, it is best to check the label.

QUICK TIP: Tamari contains less than half the sodium of soy sauce and is sweeter, with a more pronounced umami flavor.

Toasted Sesame Oil

This nutty-flavored toasted oil can be very mild, or it can be infused with hot chiles and called hot sesame oil. It is usually added near the end of the process to flavor the stir-fry.

QUICK TIP: Do not use sesame oil as your stir-fry cooking oil, as it burns easily.

Refrigerator Staples

To take your stir-fry flavor to the next level, you will also need to stock your refrigerator with aromatics and sauces. See my must-haves below, as well as some quick tips on how to make the most of them.

Black Bean Sauce

This sauce is made with fermented soybeans, garlic, ginger, soy sauce, and broth, resulting in a rich sauce for finishing and glazing stir-fry dishes.

QUICK TIP: Lee Kum Kee Black Bean Sauce is available in the international section of most grocery stores and Asian markets. It stores well in the refrigerator for up to a year.

Ginger

Ginger is a key component of the Chinese flavor base, along with garlic and scallions. You can buy it fresh in most grocery stores, and there's no need to peel it. In addition to its unique flavor, ginger has many health benefits including anti-nausea and anti-inflammatory effects. It is often crushed and brewed into tea with some honey or sugar to help with digestion and immune response. Dry, ground ginger is much more concentrated than fresh. For 1 tablespoon of fresh ginger (about 1 square inch), use ¼ teaspoon dried.

QUICK TIP: Choose fresh ginger with a smooth skin. You can store it in a resealable plastic bag and refrigerate for up to a week.

Gochujang

This Korean spicy-sweet fermented sauce is made from glutinous rice, soybeans, and chiles, and is an excellent marinade and finishing sauce. It can also be combined with vinegar, wine, and soy sauce as a dipping sauce.

QUICK TIP: Gochujang is in the international section of some supermarkets. It is also readily available in Asian markets and on Amazon. Gochujang stores well in the refrigerator for up to a year.

Kimchi

Kimchi is basically spicy Korean sauerkraut that was invented over 2,000 years ago as a way of preserving vegetables. Kimchi is considered the national food of Korea. More than 1.5 billion pounds are eaten every year, and there are over 100 varieties of this healthy fermented side dish. When posing for photographs, Koreans say "Kimchi!" instead of "Cheese!"

QUICK TIP: Kimchi can be stored covered at room temperature for up to a week or in your refrigerator for three to six months. It will continue to ferment and will gradually become softer and more sour.

Oyster Sauce

Oyster sauce was invented by accident in the 1800s when Guangdong street vendor Lee Kum Sheung forgot he had a pot of oyster soup simmering on the back burner of his cart. By the time he remembered it, the oyster soup had cooked down to a sweet, dark sauce. Lee's discovery helped him launch Lee Kum Kee, one of the largest food companies in the world today.

QUICK TIP: Oyster sauce can be combined with soy sauce, vinegar, wine, and sesame oil for dips, dressings, and marinades.

Scallions

Scallions are one of the key components of the Chinese flavor base, along with ginger and garlic. They are the younger shoots of green and spring onions. All parts are edible, with the white part having a stronger onion flavor than the green shoots. In many recipes in this book, you'll see an instruction to "bruise" the scallions by squeezing them before adding to the dish; this releases their aroma and flavor.

QUICK TIP: If you save and place the last inch of the white bulb with small roots in water or soil, you can grow new scallions in a couple of weeks.

Tofu

Tofu is known by some as vegan cheese. Instead of cow, goat, or sheep milk, tofu is made from soy milk, which is curdled using vinegar or citrus juice, rather than rennet from cows' stomachs. Like cheese, there are many varieties of tofu, each processed and aged differently.

QUICK TIP: Extra-firm tofu is best for stir-frying. If you want even firmer tofu, you can slice the tofu, then freeze, thaw, and drain it before stir-frying.

SOY SAUCE, A FOUNDATIONAL FLAVOR

Soy sauce originated in China over 3,000 years ago when a fermented sauce of fish, meat, grains, water, and salt was used as a preservative. The unique umami flavor of the sauce comes from the introduction of a mold, aspergillus. Two thousand years ago, more plentiful soybeans replaced the other ingredients. This sauce, called jiangyou, was the first soy sauce. Over time, soy sauce expanded to Korea and Japan. The English term "soy sauce" comes from the Japanese name for it, shoyu. From East Asia, the production of soy sauce expanded across the world, with each culture putting its own spin on the original. It was introduced to Europe by English traders in the 1700s and became a key ingredient in Worcestershire sauce. It is also a major ingredient in Switzerland's Maggi sauce, developed in the 1800s.

There are three grades of soy sauce. Regular soy sauce is the thinnest and saltiest and is used in most recipes. Sometimes called light soy sauce, it should not be confused with low-sodium soy sauce. Dark soy sauce is slightly thicker, less salty, and a little sweet. It is used as a marinade or in dips. Thick soy sauce is almost a paste and is very sweet. It is used for roasting meats and as a glaze at the end of stir-frying.

A versatile sauce, soy sauce can be drizzled into the wok at the very end to give the stir-fry extra flavor. It is also great as a marinade either alone or combined with other sauces and spices. Combined with cornstarch, it makes a glaze or gravy. There are even flavored soy sauces you can buy, such as mushroom, garlic, ginger, smoked, and more.

A Cook's Dozen Tips for Stir-Fry Success

To get you ready and excited to start your stir-fry journey, here are 12 tips to guide you to stir-fry success.

Read the recipe twice. This will give you the opportunity to gather tools, check ingredients, and rehearse the cooking process.

Use room-temperature ingredients. For thousands of years, cooks did not have refrigeration. Original recipes called for fresh ingredients. Cold ingredients will cool the wok, slowing the stir-frying process.

Prep all your ingredients before heating your wok. Stir-frying requires minute-to-minute timing. Once stir-frying begins, there is no time to find and prep ingredients, so have everything ready before you start!

Cut ingredients into "chopstick-size" pieces. Bite-size pieces cook quickly and evenly in a stir-fry. Sliced ingredients provide multiple surfaces for marinating, searing, and sealing in flavor.

Arrange ingredients in cooking order. By organizing the ingredients, you'll be prepared to add them to the wok quickly. By putting the ingredients in order, you essentially rehearse the recipe. Plus, guests will be impressed by how organized and relaxed you are while cooking.

Choose a well-seasoned wok or a large, heavy skillet. A well-seasoned cast iron or carbon steel wok with a rounded bottom will be your most effective choice. A flat-bottomed wok or Asian stir-fry pan is a good second choice. A cast-iron, carbon, or stainless-steel skillet can work almost as well but will not have the same capacity as a wok of the same diameter. Additionally, due to the skillet's large, flat bottom, you'll need more oil to keep food from sticking and burning. See page 3 for more information on choosing your wok.

Preheat your wok before adding any ingredients. Stir-frying sears ingredients quickly at a high temperature, so your wok must be at the correct temperature before adding ingredients. You will know the well-seasoned wok is hot enough to begin stir-frying when it just begins to smoke. That is when you should add the oil (not before), followed quickly by aromatics such as ginger and garlic. If you are using a new wok or an unseasoned skillet, you can test for readiness by flicking drops of water into the pan. If the drops sizzle before evaporating, it's time to stir-fry.

Choose the correct oil. Use oil that won't break down at high temperatures. Suitable oils are avocado, peanut, soybean, safflower, canola, coconut, and sunflower. For even more authentic flavor, try stir-frying with lard (pig fat), tallow (beef fat), or schmaltz (chicken fat). After you add the oil to the preheated wok, you'll want to coat the pan at least halfway up the sides with the oil. There are two ways to accomplish this: lift and tilt the wok to move the oil up and around the sides, or use your spoon or spatula to spread the oil.

Add ingredients according to cook time. Ingredients that take longer to cook should be stir-fried first, so that they continue to cook while subsequent ingredients are added. If you're using carrots, onions, and shrimp, start with the carrots. Then add the onions, followed by the shrimp. By the time you've cooked the onions and the shrimp, the carrots will be done, too. A note on preparing carrots and other root vegetables for stir-frying: A roll cut helps root vegetables cook faster by exposing more surface area to the heat of the wok. Roll-cut carrots into uniform ½-inch pieces by first cutting the end of the carrot at a 45-degree angle, then rolling the carrot a quarter turn and cutting a ½-inch piece again at an angle.

Maintain the sizzle. Do not overload your wok. Doing so will lower its temperature, interrupting the stir-frying process. If you add wet or cold ingredients and the loud sizzling stops, you've overloaded the wok. You'll need to empty it and start over again.

Keep things moving. Stir-frying happens by tossing ingredients with oil in a hot wok, searing and caramelizing their natural sugars. Stirring keeps things from getting too hot, sticking, and burning. If possible, you should maintain good ventilation with an exhaust fan and/or an open window. This is especially important when adding hot peppers! When adding hot peppers, either reduce the heat to prevent smoking or only add hot peppers along with liquids or other ingredients to minimize the chance of burning; if hot peppers burn, the smoke can be very irritating, so it's a good idea to increase ventilation (turn on a stove fan or open a window).

Add sauces at the end. Remember that stir-frying is a "dry" process, using oil to sear and brown ingredients. Adding a wet sauce lowers the temperature, stopping the stir-frying process.

Serve and eat ASAP! Stir-fry is best just as it finishes cooking in the wok. The next best thing is to have a bowl of steaming rice or noodles ready to top off with heaps of fresh, hot, juicy stir-fry.

PERFECT RICE RECIPES

Stir-frying is the most common cooking method in Asia—and rice is the most common grain, making stir-fry and rice the perfect combination! I recommend serving all recipes in this book with rice. Although there are thousands of rice varieties across Asia, grocery stores typically carry just a handful. Asian markets carry half a dozen more. Read on to learn how to prepare a small variety of rice for your next stir-fry.

The easiest path to perfect rice is a rice cooker. Measure your rice and water and push a button—it's that easy! Fancy cookers let you select what kind of rice you're preparing, and some will even play a cute song when the rice is ready.

If you don't have a rice cooker, steaming rice works well too. The key word here is steaming. Recall eighth-grade science class, when you learned that steam under pressure can exceed water's boiling temperature of 212°F (we all remember that, right?). You want to maintain a head of steam when cooking rice. Do not lift the cover while the rice is cooking! Lifting the lid to check or stir the rice allows steam to escape, resulting in mushy, incompletely cooked rice.

Below are some recipes for different types of rice. The basic recipe is for my mom's perfect steamed white rice. It works for all types of white rice including Chinese long-grain, Thai jasmine, Indian basmati, and Japanese short-grain sushi rice.

White Rice

1. Use between ⅓ and ½ cup uncooked rice per person. The cooked rice will double in volume.

2. Place the rice in a heavy pot that is 3 to 4 times the volume of the uncooked rice.

3. Add enough water to submerge the rice so that when you touch the top of the rice with the tip of your index finger, the water just covers the first joint on your finger. Experience will help determine the exact level.

4. Bring the water and rice to a boil on high heat.

5. Once boiling, switch the heat to the lowest setting and cover the rice with a heavy lid.

CONTINUED >

6. Wait for 15 minutes before checking the rice. I repeat: Do not lift the lid for 15 minutes! Turn the heat off.

7. Serve as is, or fluff with a fork and top with fresh stir-fry. You can leave the rice covered, and it will keep warm for 30 to 45 minutes.

Sticky Rice

You can find sticky rice, sometimes called "sweet rice" or "glutinous rice," in the international section of some supermarkets, in Asian markets, and online. Although referred to as "glutinous rice," sticky rice is gluten-free. Glutinous simply refers to its stickiness. You can prepare sticky rice similarly to white rice with a couple of key adjustments:

In step 3, you will want to add a little less water. Use your pinky finger rather than your index finger to measure water up to the first joint of your finger.

In step 6, you will want to turn off the heat after 10 minutes, but wait 15 more minutes before looking in to check the rice. The residual heat and steam will gently cook the sticky rice.

Brown Rice

Unlike white rice, brown rice still has its outer bran covering. The recipe for brown rice is like white rice with just two changes:

In step 3, you will want to use a little more water. Use your thumb to measure the water rather than your index finger, and add water until it reaches the first joint of your thumb.

In step 6, you will need to wait 40 minutes for the rice to be fully steamed before lifting the cover.

Finally, another great way to add variety to your rice is to cook it in flavored liquids. Just follow the instructions for the type of rice you prefer and substitute coconut water, broth, or your favorite tea for water. One tea I recommend for making rice is Lapsang souchong, a strong smoked black tea from the Fujian region of southern China. It imparts a wonderful wood-smoked flavor to the rice. Some compare its flavor to a fine smoky whiskey.

Stir-Fry Your Own Creations

Stir-fry was invented in China and has spread around the world as travelers to and from China shared meals. The basics of stir-frying are easily adapted to the flavors and ingredients of both surrounding and distant countries. Japan, Thailand, Vietnam, Malaysia, the Philippines, Indonesia, and India are just a few of the many countries that adopted stir-fry. In the United States, Chinese-American cooks invented recipes unknown in China, or changed them for the American palate. There is no Orange Beef in China, and General Tso's Chicken tastes very different in the United States than in its native Taiwan.

Stir-frying is so quick and simple that it is easily adapted to include any combination of flavors and ingredients to suit your palate. It shares many characteristics with other types of cooking around the world. For example, the filling for Mexican fajitas is a mix of sliced meat and vegetables cooked quickly over high heat in a steel pan, much like stir-fry. As you become more comfortable with stir-fry, you may want to experiment with your own flavors and ingredients. Who knows, there could be Mexican, Italian, Greek, or even Polish stir-fry in your future! I've included a Cook Time Cheat Sheet (page 150) and a Flavor Base by Country sheet (page 155) in the back of this book so you can get started experimenting with combinations of your favorite ingredients and flavor profiles.

Hot and Sour Seafood Soup [page 65]

Korean Vegetables with Gochujang [page 36]

[THREE]

VEGETABLES, TOFU & EGGS

VEGETABLES, TOFU & EGGS

With a couple of exceptions, the stir-fry recipes in this chapter are built around non-meat ingredients. While stir-fry techniques vary across borders, there are usually many types of vegetables featured in each of the dishes. What distinguishes each country's recipes are the unique tastes and smells created by the spices and aromatics making up the flavor base specific to that culture. The Cantonese flavor base of ginger, garlic, and scallions gives southern Chinese stir-fry a mildly sweet and pungent taste. Spicy curry, lime, and strong-smelling fish sauce lend their zesty, tangy flavors to Thai stir-fry. Indian stir-fry brings together onions, garlic, and cumin for a fragrant, earthy base. Although stir-fry began in China, as it spread many flavor bases blended. You will recognize those connections as you make these recipes. Hopefully you'll experiment and create your own favorite flavor foundations!

CANTONESE VEGETABLES

SERVES: 4   **PREP TIME:** 15 minutes   **COOK TIME:** 6 minutes

This hearty vegetable stir-fry features the ginger, garlic, and scallion flavor base of southern China's Canton province, now called the Guangdong province. Many Chinese immigrants to America in the 1800s opened restaurants to make a living and to feed their newly formed communities. This quick, tasty, and inexpensive dish introduced many Americans to southern-style Chinese food.

- ¼ cup soy sauce
- 1 tablespoon cornstarch
- 1 tablespoon brown sugar
- 2 tablespoons cooking oil
- 1 medium carrot, roll-cut into ½-inch pieces
- 1 tablespoon crushed, chopped ginger
- 2 garlic cloves, crushed and chopped
- 1 medium onion, quartered and cut into 1-inch pieces
- 1 cup sliced mushrooms
- 1 medium red bell pepper, cut into 1-inch pieces
- 1 cup 1-inch cut bok choy or Chinese cabbage
- 4 scallions, cut diagonally into 1-inch slices

1. In a small bowl, whisk together the soy sauce, cornstarch, and brown sugar to form a roux. Set aside.
2. In a wok over high heat, heat the cooking oil until it shimmers.
3. Add the carrot, ginger, and garlic and stir-fry for 1 minute.
4. Add the onion and mushrooms and stir-fry for 1 minute.
5. Add the bell pepper and stir-fry for 1 minute.
6. Add the bok choy and toss with the other ingredients.
7. Add the roux and mix until a light glaze forms.
8. Toss in the scallions. Serve immediately over steamed rice.

VIETNAMESE VEGETABLES WITH FISH SAUCE

SERVES: 4   **PREP TIME:** 15 minutes   **COOK TIME:** 5 minutes

Vietnamese food is noted for its fresh, lightly cooked ingredients with little oil, along with the salty, umami-flavored fish sauce used in many dishes. The fresh chiles provide just a touch of heat. The easiest way to slice hot peppers for stir-frying is to cut them crosswise, making ⅛- to ¼-inch rings. It is not necessary to remove the core or the seeds. Just be sure to avoid touching your face or eyes after preparing them, and wash your hands with soap afterward.

- 1 tablespoon cooking oil
- 3 scallions, minced
- 1 medium red onion, diced
- 2 garlic cloves, crushed and chopped
- 1 cup sliced mushrooms
- 1 chile, cut crosswise, into ⅛- to ¼-inch rings
- 2 cups sugar snap or snow pea pods
- 1 cup ¼-inch sliced Napa cabbage
- 2 tablespoons fish sauce
- 2 tablespoons rice wine
- ¼ teaspoon ground white pepper
- ½ cup coarsely chopped cilantro, parsley, dill, or mint

1. In a wok over high heat, heat the cooking oil until it shimmers.
2. Add the scallions, onion, and garlic and stir-fry for 30 seconds.
3. Add the mushrooms and stir-fry for 30 seconds.
4. Add the chile and stir-fry for 30 seconds.
5. Add the pea pods and stir-fry for 30 seconds.
6. Add the cabbage and stir-fry for 30 seconds.
7. Toss the fish sauce, rice wine, and white pepper with the vegetables for 30 seconds.
8. Serve over steamed rice or noodles, topped with the fresh herbs of your choice.

INGREDIENT TIP: *You can regulate the spiciness of this recipe by using more or less chile. You can also use black pepper. White pepper is hotter, but black pepper has a more complex flavor because it includes the outer covering of the peppercorn.*

THAI VEGETABLES WITH BASIL

SERVES: 4   **PREP TIME:** 15 minutes   **COOK TIME:** 6 minutes

Thai and Vietnamese stir-fries share some flavors and ingredients, with a few key differences. Both cuisines use garlic, limes, and fish sauce. You can use Thai and Vietnamese fish sauce interchangeably, but Thai fish sauce is saltier and more concentrated in flavor. Thai dishes also use spicy hot curries, curry paste, and dried peppers, while Vietnamese foods use milder fresh peppers.

- 2 tablespoons red Thai curry paste
- 2 tablespoons fish sauce
- 1 teaspoon hot sesame oil
- Juice of 1 lime
- 3 tablespoons brown sugar

- 1 tablespoon cornstarch
- 2 tablespoons cooking oil
- 2 garlic cloves, crushed and chopped
- 1 medium carrot, roll-cut into ½-inch pieces
- 1 medium onion, cut into 1-inch pieces

- 2 cups sugar snap or snow pea pods
- 1 red bell pepper, cut into 1-inch pieces
- 2 cups basil leaves
- 1 cup fresh bean sprouts
- ½ cup chopped cilantro

1. In a small bowl, whisk together the curry paste, fish sauce, sesame oil, lime juice, brown sugar, and cornstarch. Set aside.
2. In a wok over high heat, heat the cooking oil until it shimmers.
3. Add the garlic and carrot and stir-fry for 1 minute.
4. Add the onion and stir-fry for 1 minute.
5. Add the pea pods and stir-fry for 1 minute.
6. Add the bell pepper and stir-fry for 1 minute.
7. Add the curry paste mixture and stir until it forms a glaze.
8. Add the basil and toss for 30 seconds until it wilts.
9. Serve over rice or noodles, topped with the bean sprouts and cilantro.

CHANGE IT UP: *For a more intense flavor, grate lime, lemon, or orange zest into the curry paste mixture before adding it to the stir-fry.*

JAPANESE STIR-FRIED VEGETABLES (YASAI ITAME)

SERVES: 4   **PREP TIME:** 15 minutes   **COOK TIME:** 6 minutes

Japanese stir-fry is as delicate and subtle as Chinese Sichuan stir-fry is fiery-hot and strongly seasoned. The milder, umami flavors of fermented miso, the sweetness of mirin wine, and the lighter saltiness of Japanese tamari soy sauce characterize the Japanese flavor base. Yasai itame means "stir-fried vegetables" in Japanese.

- 2 tablespoons yellow miso
- 2 tablespoons mirin
- 2 tablespoons tamari
- 1 tablespoon toasted sesame oil
- 2 tablespoons cooking oil

- 1 tablespoon crushed, chopped ginger
- 2 garlic cloves, crushed and chopped
- 1 medium carrot, roll-cut into ½-inch pieces
- 1 medium onion, cut into 1-inch pieces

- 4 ounces shiitake mushrooms, cut into slices
- 1 red bell pepper, cut into 1-inch pieces
- 4 scallions, cut into 1-inch pieces
- 2 cups bean sprouts

1. In a small bowl, whisk together the miso, mirin, tamari, and sesame oil. Set aside.
2. In a wok over high heat, heat the cooking oil until it shimmers.
3. Add the ginger, garlic, and carrot and stir-fry for 1 minute.
4. Add the onion and mushrooms and stir-fry for 1 minute.
5. Add the bell pepper and scallions and stir-fry for 1 minute.
6. Add the miso mixture and toss for 30 seconds.
7. Serve with steamed Japanese rice and garnish with bean sprouts.

FILIPINO VEGETABLES WITH OYSTER SAUCE

SERVES: 4   **PREP TIME:** 15 minutes   **COOK TIME:** 6 minutes

Filipino stir-fry is unique because it brings together the flavors of Europe and Asia. The Spanish sofrito flavor base of garlic, onion, and tomato is the legacy of hundreds of years of Spanish colonization in the Philippines. Likewise, the flavors of soy sauce, ginger, and oyster sauce were introduced in the country by Chinese pirates and traders. With the Philippines at the crossroads of Europe and Asia, Filipino food may have been the first East-West fusion cuisine!

- 2 tablespoons cooking oil
- 2 garlic cloves, crushed and chopped
- 1 tablespoon crushed, chopped ginger
- 1 medium carrot, roll-cut into ½-inch pieces
- 1 medium onion, diced
- 12 cherry tomatoes, cut in half
- 2 cups sugar snap or snow pea pods
- 1 red bell pepper, cut into 1-inch pieces
- ¼ cup oyster sauce
- 2 tablespoons soy sauce

1. In a wok over high heat, heat the cooking oil until it shimmers.
2. Add the garlic, ginger, and carrot and stir-fry for 1 minute.
3. Add the onion and stir-fry for 1 minute.
4. Add the cherry tomatoes and stir-fry for 1 minute.
5. Add the pea pods and bell pepper and stir-fry for 1 minute.
6. Add the oyster sauce and soy sauce and stir until a light glaze forms.
7. Serve over steamed rice.

PREPARATION TIP: *Use the flat side of your cleaver or chef's knife to crush your garlic before chopping it. Crushing aromatics like ginger and garlic quickly releases more of the aroma and flavor. For ginger, cut across the grain first, then crush it with the side of your knife.*

INDIAN FIVE-SPICE VEGETABLES

SERVES: 4   **PREP TIME:** 15 minutes   **COOK TIME:** 6 minutes

India is known for its wide variety of curry mixes. There are dozens of different ingredients that can be used to create curries, making the possible combinations virtually limitless. However, there are five ingredients that are most often used in curries: cumin, coriander, cloves, turmeric, and fennel.

- 2 tablespoons cooking oil
- 2 garlic cloves, crushed and chopped
- 1 medium carrot, roll-cut into ½-inch pieces
- 1 medium onion, cut into 1-inch pieces
- 2 cups sugar snap pea pods
- 1 medium poblano pepper, cut into 1-inch pieces
- 1 red bell pepper, cut into 1-inch pieces
- 4 scallions, cut into 1-inch slices
- ¼ teaspoon ground cumin
- ¼ teaspoon ground coriander
- ¼ teaspoon ground cloves
- ¼ teaspoon ground turmeric
- ¼ teaspoon ground fennel
- 1 teaspoon hot sesame oil

1. In a wok over high heat, heat the cooking oil until it shimmers.
2. Add the garlic and carrot and stir-fry for 1 minute.
3. Add the onion and stir-fry for 1 minute.
4. Add the pea pods and stir-fry for 1 minute.
5. Add the poblano and bell peppers and stir-fry for 1 minute.
6. Add the scallions and stir-fry for 30 seconds.
7. Add the cumin, coriander, cloves, turmeric, fennel, and sesame oil and stir-fry for 30 seconds.
8. Serve over steamed basmati rice.

INGREDIENT TIP: *You can substitute one teaspoon of Chinese five-spice powder plus ¼ teaspoon of cumin for the Indian five-spice mix included here. Cumin is generally not found in five-spice powder, so it is unique to this recipe.*

KOREAN VEGETABLES WITH GOCHUJANG

SERVES: 4   **PREP TIME:** 15 minutes   **COOK TIME:** 6 minutes

Fermented Korean pepper paste , or gochujang, has been used since the ninth century as a medicine. It wasn't until the 16th century that the red fermented mixture of chile, rice, soybeans, and salt, became Korea's favorite sauce. It is so popular now that it has its own festival in Korea each year.

- 2 tablespoons cooking oil
- 1 tablespoon crushed, chopped ginger
- 2 garlic cloves, crushed and chopped
- 1 medium onion, cut into 1-inch pieces
- 4 ounces shiitake mushrooms, sliced
- 2 cups sugar snap or snow pea pods
- 1 red bell pepper, cut into 1-inch pieces
- 2 heads baby bok choy, leaves separated
- 2 tablespoons gochujang
- ½ cup kimchi
- 2 tablespoons soy sauce

1. In a wok over high heat, heat the cooking oil until it shimmers.
2. Add the ginger, garlic, and onion and stir-fry for 1 minute.
3. Add the mushrooms and stir-fry for 1 minute.
4. Add the pea pods and stir-fry for 1 minute.
5. Add the bell pepper and bok choy and stir-fry for 1 minute.
6. Add the gochujang, kimchi, and soy sauce and stir-fry for 1 minute.
7. Serve over steamed jasmine rice.

INGREDIENT TIP: *There are many varieties of kimchi. Some are very spicy, and some are very mild. Experiment with different kinds! It keeps for a month or more in the refrigerator but can get mushy over time.*

MALAYSIAN VEGETABLE CURRY

SERVES: 4   **PREP TIME:** 15 minutes   **COOK TIME:** 6 minutes

Malaysia's cuisine is a direct result of its geographical location at a maritime crossroads as well as its colonial history. Malaysian dishes have influences from China, India, Indonesia, the Middle East, Thailand, and several European countries. I remember seeing street food influenced by all these countries while exploring Malaysia's capital, Kuala Lumpur.

- 2 tablespoons soy sauce
- 1 tablespoon hot sesame oil
- 1 teaspoon Chinese five-spice powder
- ¼ teaspoon ground cumin
- ¼ teaspoon ground fennel
- ½ teaspoon ground chili powder
- 2 tablespoons coconut oil
- 1 tablespoon crushed, chopped ginger
- 1 medium carrot, roll-cut into ½-inch pieces
- 1 medium red onion, diced
- 2 cups sugar snap or snow pea pods
- ¼ cup unsweetened and shredded dried coconut

1. In a small bowl, whisk together the soy sauce, sesame oil, five-spice powder, cumin, fennel, and chili powder. Set aside.
2. In a wok over high heat, heat the coconut oil until it shimmers.
3. Add the ginger and carrot and stir-fry for 1 minute.
4. Add the onion and stir-fry for 1 minute.
5. Add the pea pods and the soy sauce mixture and stir-fry for 1 minute.
6. Add the coconut and stir-fry for 1 minute.
7. Serve over steamed rice made with coconut water or coconut milk.

MYANMARESE VEGETABLES WITH HOT PEPPERS

SERVES: 4　　　　　**PREP TIME:** 15 minutes　　　　　**COOK TIME:** 6 minutes

Although Myanmarese cuisine has been influenced by surrounding countries, it is typically not as hot as Thai, less spicy than Indian, and only like Chinese in its vegetable stir-fry. The former capital of Myanmar, Yangon, also known as Rangoon, lent its name to the popular Chinese-American appetizer, crab rangoon.

- 1 teaspoon hot sesame oil
- Juice of 1 lime
- 1 tablespoon fish sauce
- 1 tablespoon Chinese five-spice powder
- 2 tablespoons cooking oil
- 2 garlic cloves, crushed and chopped
- 1 medium carrot, roll-cut into ½-inch pieces
- 2-3 red chiles, cut into ¼-inch pieces
- 2 cups sugar snap or snow pea pods
- 1 red bell pepper, cut into 1-inch pieces
- 1 small mango, peeled and cut into ½-inch pieces
- 2 baby bok choy, leaves separated

1. In a small bowl, whisk together the sesame oil, lime juice, fish sauce, and five-spice powder. Set aside.
2. In a wok over high heat, heat the cooking oil until it shimmers.
3. Add the garlic and carrot and stir-fry for 1 minute.
4. Add the chiles and stir-fry for 30 seconds.
5. Add the pea pods and bell pepper and stir-fry for 1 minute.
6. Add the mango and stir-fry for 1 minute, then add the sesame oil mixture.
7. Add the bok choy and stir-fry for 1 minute.
8. Serve over steamed jasmine rice.

INGREDIENT TIP: *Look for a mango that is somewhat firm for this recipe. A soft mango will not hold up as well when stir-fried.*

BUDDHA'S DELIGHT

SERVES: 4   PREP TIME: 15 minutes   COOK TIME: 8 minutes

This is a classic Buddhist vegetarian dish with many variations, all of them meat-less. It is traditionally served on the first day of the Chinese New Year. This dish can be as simple as two or three vegetables or as elaborate as a dozen; this version is right in the middle. Feel free to regulate the spiciness in this recipe by increasing or decreasing the amount of hot sesame oil.

- 2 tablespoons rice wine
- 2 tablespoons soy sauce or tamari
- 2 tablespoons rice vinegar
- 1 tablespoon hot sesame oil
- 1 tablespoon Chinese five-spice powder
- 1 tablespoon cornstarch

- ¼ cup cooking oil
- 1 pound extra-firm tofu, well drained, patted dry, and cut into bite-size pieces
- 1 tablespoon crushed, chopped ginger
- 3 garlic cloves, crushed and chopped

- 1 medium carrot, roll-cut into ½-inch pieces
- 4 ounces mushrooms, cut into slices
- 1 red bell pepper, cut into 1-inch pieces
- 1 dozen sugar snap or snow pea pods
- 4 scallions, cut into 1-inch pieces

1. In a small bowl, whisk together the rice wine, soy sauce, rice vinegar, sesame oil, five-spice powder, and cornstarch. Set aside.
2. In a wok over high heat, heat the cooking oil until it shimmers.
3. Add the tofu, ginger, and garlic and stir-fry for 1 minute, or until the tofu begins to brown.
4. Add the carrot and stir-fry for 1 minute.
5. Add the mushrooms and stir-fry for 1 minute.
6. Add the bell pepper and stir-fry for 1 minute.
7. Add the pea pods and stir-fry for 1 minute.
8. Add the scallions and stir-fry for 30 seconds.
9. Add the rice wine mixture and stir-fry until a light glaze forms.
10. Serve over steamed rice.

MAPO TOFU

SERVES: 4 **PREP TIME:** 15 minutes **COOK TIME:** 8 minutes

It's been said that this spicy dish from the city of Chengdu in the Sichuan province of China is named after a pockmarked (ma) grandmother (po) who invented it for a traveling businessman, who then spread the word about mapo tofu in his travels. According to Mrs. Chiang's Szechwan Cookbook, *Eugene Wu, the librarian of the Harvard Yenching Library, grew up in Chengdu and claims that as a schoolboy he used to order mapo tofu at a restaurant run by the original Pock-Marked Po herself. One ordered by weight, specifying how many grams of bean curd and meat, and the serving would be weighed out and cooked as the diner watched. It's not strictly a vegetarian dish but can be made meatless if desired.*

- 2 tablespoons cooking oil
- 1 pound extra-firm tofu, cut into 1-inch pieces
- 1 tablespoon crushed, chopped ginger
- 2 garlic cloves, crushed and chopped

- ½ pound ground pork
- 4 ounces mushrooms, chopped into ¼-inch pieces
- 4 tablespoons spicy black bean sauce
- 1 tablespoon ground Sichuan peppercorns

- 1 tablespoon rice wine
- 1 teaspoon hot sesame oil
- 4 scallions, cut into 1-inch slices

1. In a wok over high heat, heat the cooking oil until it shimmers.
2. Add the tofu, ginger, and garlic and stir-fry for 1 minute.
3. Add the pork and stir-fry for 1 minute.
4. Add the mushrooms and stir-fry for 1 minute.
5. Add the black bean sauce and stir-fry for 30 seconds.
6. Add the peppercorns, rice wine, and sesame oil and stir-fry for 30 seconds.
7. Add the scallions and stir-fry for 30 seconds.
8. Serve over steamed rice.

CHANGE IT UP: *Leave out the pork for a vegetarian version of this recipe.*

TERIYAKI TOFU

SERVES: 4   **PREP TIME:** 15 minutes   **COOK TIME:** 8 minutes

In Japanese, "teriyaki" means "shining grill," which refers to the glaze produced by the combination of sweetened tamari and fast cooking on a very hot surface that caramelizes the natural and added sugars in this dish.

- ¼ cup plus 2 tablespoons tamari, divided
- 2 tablespoons mirin wine
- 2 tablespoons rice vinegar
- 2 tablespoons toasted sesame oil
- 2 tablespoons brown sugar
- 1 tablespoon white miso
- 1 tablespoon cornstarch
- 2 tablespoons cooking oil
- 1 pound extra-firm tofu, drained and cut into 1-inch cubes
- 2 garlic cloves, crushed and chopped
- 1 tablespoon crushed, chopped ginger
- 1 medium onion, cut into 1-inch pieces
- 1 red bell pepper, cut into 1-inch pieces
- 4 ounces shiitake mushrooms, cut into slices
- 2 tablespoons toasted sesame seeds

1. In a small bowl, whisk together ¼ cup of the tamari, the mirin, rice vinegar, sesame oil, brown sugar, miso, and cornstarch. Set aside.
2. In a wok over high heat, heat the cooking oil until it shimmers.
3. Add the tofu, garlic, ginger, and remaining 2 tablespoons of tamari and stir-fry for 2 minutes, or until the tofu starts to brown.
4. Add the onion and stir-fry for 1 minute.
5. Add the bell pepper and stir-fry for 1 minute.
6. Add the mushrooms and stir-fry for 1 minute.
7. Add the tamari mixture to the wok and stir-fry until a light glaze forms.
8. Sprinkle with the sesame seeds and serve over Japanese medium-grain white rice.

INGREDIENT TIP: *White miso is a Japanese paste made from fermented soybeans, salt, and rice. It has a deep umami flavor, and also comes in yellow and red variations.*

CURRIED TOFU

SERVES: 4   **PREP TIME: 15 minutes**   **COOK TIME: 8 minutes**

The "nationality" of this curried tofu is flexible depending on what type of curry you use. If you use a dry curry powder, it will be Indian-inspired. If you opt for a wet curry, it will be Thai-inspired. And if you choose Chinese five-spice powder, you'll be eating Chinese stir-fry.

- 2 tablespoons curry of choice
- 2 tablespoons rice vinegar
- 2 tablespoons soy sauce
- ½ cup vegetable or meat broth
- 2 tablespoons cornstarch

- 2 tablespoons cooking oil
- 2 garlic cloves, crushed and chopped
- 1 tablespoon crushed, chopped ginger
- 1 pound extra-firm tofu, well drained, patted dry, and cut into 1-inch pieces

- 1 medium carrot, roll-cut into ½-inch pieces
- 1 medium onion, cut into 1-inch pieces
- 4 ounces mushrooms, cut into slices
- 1 red bell pepper, cut into 1-inch pieces

1. In a small bowl, whisk together the curry, rice vinegar, soy sauce, broth, and cornstarch. Set aside.

2. In a wok over high heat, heat the cooking oil until it shimmers.

3. Add the garlic, ginger, and tofu and stir-fry for 2 minutes, or until the tofu begins to brown.

4. Add the carrot and stir-fry for 1 minute.

5. Add the onion and stir-fry for 1 minute.

6. Add the mushrooms and stir-fry for 1 minute.

7. Add the bell pepper and stir-fry for 1 minute.

8. Add the curry mixture to the wok and stir-fry until a glaze forms.

9. Serve over basmati (Indian), coconut jasmine (Thai), or long-grain white rice (Chinese), depending on the type of curry you used.

CHANGE IT UP: *Rice is the most common starch across Asia. Delicate long-grain basmati rice goes well with pungent Indian flavors, while the sweet fragrance of jasmine rice cooked in coconut water or coconut milk blends well with the heat of Thai curry. Basic Chinese white rice allows the licorice flavor of star anise in five-spice powder to shine. For variety, you can mix rice types and curries as you wish!*

GARLIC EGGS AND VEGETABLES

SERVES: 4   **PREP TIME:** 15 minutes   **COOK TIME:** 8 minutes

Woks are great for stir-frying eggs. The rounded bottom is made for scrambling them quickly with a minimal amount of oil. Combined with fresh vegetables, wok-scrambled eggs make a fast snack, side dish, or meal.

- 2 tablespoons cooking oil
- 3 garlic cloves, crushed and chopped
- 6 eggs, beaten
- 2 tablespoons rice wine
- 3 scallions, cut into ½-inch pieces
- 1 cup chopped bok choy
- 2 tablespoons soy sauce
- ¼ cup hoisin sauce

1. In a wok over high heat, heat the cooking oil until it shimmers.
2. Add the garlic and stir-fry for 10 to 15 seconds or until lightly browned.
3. Add the eggs and rice wine and stir-fry until the eggs are firm but still moist.
4. Add the scallions and stir-fry for 30 seconds.
5. Add the bok choy and stir-fry for 1 minute.
6. In a small bowl, combine the soy sauce and hoisin sauce. Drizzle over the scrambled eggs. Serve alone or over steamed rice.

VARIATION TIP: *Soft or silken tofu can be substituted for the eggs for a vegan recipe; use 1½ cups tofu to equal 6 eggs.*

STIR-FRIED VEGETABLE, EGG, AND TOFU SOUP

SERVES: 4   PREP TIME: 15 minutes   COOK TIME: 8 minutes

The high heat of stir-frying releases the flavors of the ingredients being cooked. Those flavors create wonderful aromas that are perfectly captured in the universal comfort food: soup! Here's a delicious vegetable, egg, and tofu soup that begins as a stir-fry.

- 2 tablespoons cooking oil
- 2 garlic cloves, crushed and chopped
- 1 tablespoon crushed, chopped ginger
- 1 pound tofu, well drained, patted dry, and cut into 1-inch pieces
- 1 red bell pepper, cut into ¼-inch pieces
- 4 ounces mushrooms, cut into slices
- 1 cup chopped bok choy
- 1 teaspoon hot sesame oil
- 2 quarts vegetable or meat broth
- 4 eggs, beaten

1. In a wok over high heat, heat the cooking oil until it shimmers.
2. Add the garlic, ginger, and tofu and stir-fry until the tofu begins to brown.
3. Add the bell pepper and stir-fry for 1 minute.
4. Add the mushrooms and stir-fry for 30 seconds.
5. Add the bok choy and stir-fry for 30 seconds.
6. Add the sesame oil, then add the broth and bring to a boil.
7. Drizzle the beaten eggs over the broth and let the eggs float to the top. Serve the soup hot as an appetizer or main dish.

Korean Spicy Squid Stir-fry [page 56]

[FOUR]

SEAFOOD

SEAFOOD

Archaeological evidence shows that seafood has been harvested in Asia for more than 40,000 years. Aquaculture appeared around the same time as the wok in China. Maybe it's a coincidence, but stir-frying's high heat and rapid searing of ingredients makes it a perfect method for cooking seafood. Searing seals in the juices and preserves the taste and texture of fresh seafood. The qualities of Asian aromatics such as ginger, garlic, and scallions go well with the sweet and subtle flavors of seafood, and the hot oil's ability to infuse and integrate the flavors makes stir-fried seafood dishes some of the world's favorite recipes.

However, when it comes to stir-frying, all fish are not created equal. It is important to choose fish fillets that can stand up to being stirred and tossed around in the wok. Avoid thin, flat fish like flounder and sole, and stick to firmer, thick cuts of cod, haddock, salmon, swordfish, and tuna.

SHRIMP WITH LOBSTER SAUCE

SERVES: 4   **PREP TIME:** 15 minutes   **COOK TIME:** 8 minutes

This is a favorite dish in many Chinese-American restaurants. It was originally known as Cantonese-Style Lobster, with lobster used as the main component of the dish as well as in the sauce. As lobster got more expensive, the crustacean was dropped from the dish and replaced with shrimp, but the name retained the "lobster." It's similar to how there's no duck in duck sauce!

- 1 cup chicken stock
- 2 tablespoons cornstarch
- 2 tablespoons soy sauce
- 1 teaspoon hot sesame oil
- 1 teaspoon sugar
- 2 tablespoons cooking oil
- 3 garlic cloves, crushed and chopped
- 1 tablespoon crushed, chopped ginger
- ½ pound ground pork
- ½ pound medium shrimp, peeled and deveined
- 1 tablespoon rice wine
- ½ cup thawed frozen peas
- 2 large eggs, beaten
- 4 scallions, cut into ½-inch pieces

1. In a small bowl, whisk together the stock, cornstarch, soy sauce, sesame oil, and sugar. Set aside.
2. In a wok over high heat, heat the cooking oil until it shimmers.
3. Add the garlic and ginger and stir-fry for 1 minute.
4. Add the pork and stir-fry for 1 minute.
5. Add the shrimp and rice wine and stir-fry for 1 minute.
6. Add the stock mixture to the wok and stir until it thickens and forms a light glaze.
7. Add the peas and drizzle in the eggs. Let the eggs poach for 1 minute before stirring gently.
8. Garnish with the scallions. Serve over steamed rice.

CHANGE IT UP: *This recipe also works well with fresh sea scallops! Of course, if you're feeling fancy, you can use lobster, too. Simply use a half-pound of whatever seafood you're substituting in place of the shrimp.*

SICHUAN SHRIMP AND MUSSELS

SERVES: 4   **PREP TIME:** 15 minutes   **COOK TIME:** 6 minutes

This is a fast, fiery dish that makes use of hot sesame oil, red pepper flakes, and mouth-numbing Sichuan peppercorns. If you prefer less heat, simply reduce the amount of any of these ingredients. You will need a cover for your wok or pan for this dish.

- 2 tablespoons cooking oil
- 4 garlic cloves, crushed and chopped
- 2 tablespoons crushed, chopped ginger
- ½ pound large shrimp, with or without shells
- ¼ cup rice wine
- 1 tablespoon red pepper flakes
- 2 tablespoons Chinese five-spice powder
- ¼ cup vegetable or meat broth
- 1 pound mussels, cleaned and rinsed
- ¼ cup oyster sauce

1. In a wok over high heat, heat the cooking oil until it shimmers.
2. Add the garlic and ginger and stir-fry until lightly browned.
3. Add the shrimp and stir-fry for 1 minute.
4. Add the rice wine, red pepper, five-spice powder, and broth and bring to a boil.
5. Add the mussels, cover the wok, and cook for 2 minutes, or until the mussels open.
6. Uncover the wok and stir the ingredients for 1 minute, mixing well.
7. Drizzle the oyster sauce over the mussels and shrimp. Serve alone or over a bed of rice on a platter or in a shallow bowl.

INGREDIENT TIP: *Tap on the shell of any open, uncooked mussels. If the shell doesn't close, discard it. Discard any unopened mussels after cooking.*

THAI FISH AND VEGETABLES

SERVES: 4   **PREP TIME:** 15 minutes   **COOK TIME:** 8 minutes

The rich, umami flavor of fish sauce, the citrusy tang of lime and lemongrass, the zing of hot peppers—all these flavors come together for a characteristically Thai dish. Use the white fish of your choice such as cod, hake, sea bass, or tilapia. Just make sure it is firm enough to stand up to the wok.

- 1 tablespoon fish sauce
- 1 tablespoon mirin
- 2 tablespoons rice vinegar
- 2 tablespoons brown sugar
- Juice of 1 lime
- 1 tablespoon cornstarch

- 1 pound fresh, firm white fish fillet, cut into 1-inch pieces
- 2 tablespoons cooking oil
- 2 garlic cloves, crushed and chopped
- 1 tablespoon crushed, chopped ginger
- 1 bruised lower stalk of lemongrass, outer leaves removed and stalk cut into 1-inch pieces

- 1 onion, cut into 1-inch pieces
- 3 Thai bird's eye chiles, cut into ¼-inch pieces
- 2 cups chopped bok choy
- 4 scallions, cut into 1-inch pieces
- 1 cup bean sprouts

1. In a large bowl, whisk together the fish sauce, mirin, rice vinegar, brown sugar, lime juice, and cornstarch.

2. Add the fish to the bowl and set aside to marinate while preparing the wok.

3. In a wok over high heat, heat the cooking oil until it shimmers.

4. Add the garlic, ginger, lemongrass, and onion and stir-fry for 1 minute.

5. Remove the lemongrass and discard.

6. Add the bird's eye chiles and stir-fry for 30 seconds.

7. Add the marinated fish to the wok, reserving the marinade, and gently stir-fry for 1 minute.

8. Add the bok choy and remaining marinade and gently stir-fry for 30 seconds.

9. Squeeze the scallions to bruise them, then sprinkle over the fish.

10. Garnish with the fresh bean sprouts and serve over steamed jasmine rice.

INGREDIENT TIP: *Bird's eye chiles are very hot. Remember to reference the tips on page 19 when you're working with hot peppers, so you don't get smoke in your eyes. If you want to reduce the heat, you can use progressively milder peppers such as serrano, jalapeño, or poblano peppers, in that order. If you prefer no spiciness at all, you could use sweet bell peppers.*

TERIYAKI SALMON

SERVES: 4   **PREP TIME:** 15 minutes   **COOK TIME:** 8 minutes

This sweet, salty, and umami-flavored stir-fry makes use of three signature Japanese ingredients. Teriyaki's classic saltiness comes from tamari, a byproduct of fermenting miso. The glaze comes from honey. Miso contributes the wonderful umami flavor. For the salmon, you can use fillets with the skin on or off; just don't use the tail end.

- 2 tablespoons tamari
- 2 tablespoons honey
- 2 tablespoons mirin
- 2 tablespoons rice vinegar
- 1 tablespoon white miso
- 1 pound thick, center-cut salmon fillet, cut into 1-inch pieces
- 2 tablespoons cooking oil
- 2 garlic cloves, crushed and chopped
- 1 tablespoon crushed, chopped ginger
- 1 medium onion, diced
- 4 ounces shiitake mushrooms, cut into slices
- 2 cups sugar snap or snow pea pods
- 2 scallions, cut into 1-inch pieces
- 1 tablespoon sesame seeds

1. In a large bowl, whisk together the tamari, honey, mirin, rice vinegar, and miso. Add the salmon, making sure to coat evenly with the marinade, and set aside.

2. In a wok over high heat, heat the cooking oil until it shimmers.

3. Add the garlic, ginger, and onion and stir-fry for 1 minute.

4. Add the mushrooms and stir-fry for 1 minute.

5. Add the pea pods and stir-fry for 1 minute.

6. Add the marinated salmon, reserving the marinade, and gently stir-fry for 1 minute.

7. Add the marinade and scallions and gently stir-fry for 30 seconds.

8. Sprinkle the sesame seeds on top. Serve over steamed medium-grain Japanese rice.

CHANGE IT UP: *Here in Maine, I sometimes replace the honey with pure maple syrup for a local flavor.*

VIETNAMESE SCALLOPS AND CUCUMBERS

SERVES: 4   PREP TIME: 15 minutes   COOK TIME: 6 minutes

This stir-fry is perfect as an appetizer salad or a light main dish. The sweet and sour, lightly spicy dressing with umami flavor from the salty fish sauce goes well with the crunchy cucumbers and tender sea scallops. To prepare the cucumber, rake the skin lengthwise with a fork, then cut the cucumber into ¼-inch disks.

- ¼ cup rice wine
- ¼ cup fish sauce
- ¼ cup brown sugar
- Juice of 1 lime
- 1 pound large sea scallops, cut in half widthwise

- 2 tablespoons cooking oil
- 2 garlic cloves, crushed and chopped
- 4 scallions, cut into 1-inch pieces

- 1 European cucumber, raked and cut into ¼-inch disks
- 1 teaspoon hot sesame oil
- ¼ cup rice vinegar

1. In a large bowl, combine the rice wine, fish sauce, brown sugar, and lime juice. Add the scallops to marinate and set aside.

2. In a wok over high heat, heat the cooking oil until it shimmers.

3. Add the garlic and scallions and stir-fry for 30 seconds.

4. Add the marinated scallops, reserving the marinade, and stir-fry for 30 seconds.

5. Add the cucumber and marinade to the wok and stir-fry for 30 seconds.

6. Turn off the heat and toss the cucumbers and scallops with the sesame oil and rice vinegar. Serve alone or over jasmine rice.

INGREDIENT TIP: *Fresh, dry sea scallops are the best choice if you can get them. Scallops have a high water content, so they expand when frozen, which decreases the integrity of the meat. If you get frozen scallops, you can thaw them overnight in the refrigerator. If time is short, thaw them in their bag submerged in warm tap water.*

KOREAN SPICY SQUID STIR-FRY

SERVES: 4   **PREP TIME:** 15 minutes   **COOK TIME:** 5 minutes

The key to cooking squid is to cook it either very quickly at a high temperature or very slowly at a low temperature. Stir-frying squid should take no more than 2 minutes. The best way to tell if squid is ready is to include tentacles in your stir-fry. As soon as they curl, the squid is done. If you don't have tentacles, the rings are done just as they turn opaque.

- 2 tablespoons cooking oil
- 2 garlic cloves, crushed and chopped
- 1 tablespoon crushed, chopped ginger
- 1 medium red onion, cut into 1-inch pieces
- 4 ounces shiitake mushrooms, cut into slices
- 2 baby bok choy, leaves separated
- ½ pound small to medium squid tentacles and rings, rinsed in cold water
- 2 Thai bird's eye chiles, cut into ¼-inch circles
- 2 tablespoons soy sauce
- 2 tablespoons rice wine
- 2 tablespoons gochujang
- 2 tablespoons brown sugar
- 1 teaspoon hot sesame oil
- 1 tablespoon sesame seeds
- 4 scallions, cut into 1-inch pieces

1. In a wok over high heat, heat the cooking oil until it shimmers.
2. Add the garlic, ginger, and onion and stir-fry for 1 minute.
3. Add the mushrooms and stir-fry for 1 minute.
4. Add the bok choy and stir-fry for 1 minute.
5. Add the squid and stir-fry for 30 seconds.
6. Add the bird's eye chiles and stir-fry for 30 seconds.
7. Add the soy sauce, rice wine, gochujang, and brown sugar and stir-fry 30 seconds.
8. Add the sesame oil, sesame seeds, and scallions and stir-fry for 30 seconds.

9. Serve over jasmine rice.

INGREDIENT TIP: *Local grocers usually have, or can get, fresh, cleaned squid tentacles and rings within a week if requested. Be sure to rinse the tentacles well, as they can be gritty.*

CLAMS WITH BLACK BEAN SAUCE

SERVES: 4   **PREP TIME:** 15 minutes   **COOK TIME:** 30 minutes

This recipe uses crushed ginger and garlic as aromatics, and then uses broth to steam small clams. The black bean sauce adds a salty, earthy flavor to the finished dish. The clams used in China are a freshwater variety that are dark yellow in color and sometimes called golden or lucky clams. This recipe uses littleneck or mahogany clams, which are just as good, but mussels can also be substituted.

- 1 cup uncooked white rice
- 1 tablespoon cooking oil
- 4 garlic cloves, crushed and chopped
- 2 tablespoons crushed, chopped ginger
- ½ cup vegetable or meat broth
- 2 cups littleneck or mahogany clams, rinsed clean
- ¼ cup rice wine
- 2 tablespoons cornstarch
- 3 tablespoons black bean sauce

1. Prepare the rice as outlined on page 21.
2. In a wok over high heat, heat the cooking oil until it shimmers.
3. Add the garlic and ginger and stir-fry for 1 minute.
4. Add the broth and bring to a boil. While waiting for the broth to boil, line a serving platter with the cooked rice.
5. Add the clams to the broth, cover the pan, and let steam for 2 minutes, or until the clams open.
6. Remove the clams and place on top of the rice, leaving the broth in the wok.
7. In a small bowl, whisk together the rice wine and cornstarch. Add to the broth along with the black bean sauce. Stir until a glaze forms.
8. Drizzle the sauce over the opened clams and rice and serve.

INGREDIENT TIP: *Any uncooked clams that will not close when tapped and any that are not open after being cooked should be tossed.*

MALAYSIAN SQUID AND CELERY

SERVES: 4   PREP TIME: 15 minutes   COOK TIME: 5 minutes

This is a common dish served in Malaysian-Chinese restaurants, known locally as "red tablecloth restaurants." More informal than the white tablecloth establishments, these eateries feature round, family-style tables covered with the traditional good luck color: bright red.

- 2 tablespoons cooking oil
- 2 garlic cloves, crushed and chopped
- 3 stalks celery, cut diagonally into ¼-inch pieces
- ½ pound small to medium squid tentacles and rings, rinsed in cold water
- 2 tablespoons rice wine
- 2 chiles, cut into ¼-inch pieces
- ½ cup oyster sauce
- 1 teaspoon hot sesame oil

1. In a wok over high heat, heat the cooking oil until it shimmers.
2. Add the garlic and celery and stir-fry for 1 minute.
3. Add the squid and rice wine and stir-fry for 1 minute.
4. Add the chiles and stir-fry for 30 seconds.
5. Add the oyster sauce and sesame oil and stir-fry for 30 seconds.
6. Serve over steamed basmati coconut rice.

PREPARATION TIP: *When preparing chiles for stir-frying, it is not necessary to remove the edible seeds or the white ribs. The seeds do not contain the heat-producing capsaicin. The white ribs provide more heat than the colored part of the pepper.*

GINGER AND SCALLION KING CRAB

SERVES: 4   **PREP TIME:** 15 minutes   **COOK TIME:** 6 minutes

King crab is an important dish—crabs have 8 legs, and 8 is a lucky number in China. In Chinese the number 8 also sounds very much like the words for "wealth," "fortune," and "prosper." And if that isn't enough, king crabs are bright red, and red is the luckiest color in China, so this tasty dish is doubly lucky! Use kitchen shears to cut the crab legs into 2-inch sections, removing the joints so the sections are open at both ends. You can also split open the sections along their lengths by cutting the thinner, white part of the shell.

- 1 cup fish or lobster broth
- 2 tablespoons rice wine
- 2 tablespoons cornstarch
- 3 tablespoons cooking oil
- 2 tablespoons crushed, chopped ginger
- 3 garlic cloves, crushed and chopped
- 2 pounds king crab legs, cut into 2-inch sections and left in the shell
- ¼ cup hoisin sauce
- 4 scallions, cut into ½-inch pieces

1. In a small bowl, whisk together the broth, rice wine, and cornstarch. Set aside.

2. In a wok over high heat, heat the cooking oil until it shimmers.

3. Add the ginger and garlic and stir-fry for 1 minute.

4. Add the crab legs and stir-fry for 1 minute.

5. Add the broth mixture and stir-fry for 1 minute.

6. Add the hoisin sauce and stir-fry until a glaze forms.

7. Bruise the scallions by squeezing them, then sprinkle them into the wok to garnish the crab legs.

8. Serve alone or over steamed rice.

GARLIC-MISO COD WITH TEA RICE

SERVES: 4   **PREP TIME:** 15 minutes   **COOK TIME:** 25 minutes

This recipe is easy to shop for if you're at the market on the way home from work and want something fresh, simple, fast, and tasty. Just pick out a pound of fresh fish fillet, take it home, start your rice, and heat up your pan. By the time your rice is scooped into a plate or bowl, the fish will be done. Although any type of fish fillet will work, firmer cuts like cod, tuna, and swordfish are best.

- 1 cup uncooked rice
- 2 cups genmaicha green tea
- 2 tablespoons white miso
- 2 tablespoons tamari
- 2 tablespoons mirin

- 2 tablespoons honey
- 1 tablespoon toasted sesame oil
- 1 pound "captain's cut" (very thick) cod, cut into 4 pieces
- 2 tablespoons cooking oil

- 3 garlic cloves, crushed and chopped
- 1 tablespoon sesame seeds
- 2 scallions cut into ½-inch pieces, for garnish

1. Prepare the rice as directed on page 21, using genmaicha green tea instead of water.
2. In a large bowl, whisk together the miso, tamari, mirin, honey, and sesame oil. Add the cod and coat evenly with the marinade, then set aside.
3. In a wok over high heat, heat the cooking oil until it shimmers.
4. Add the garlic and stir-fry for 30 seconds until browned.
5. Place the marinated cod in the wok, reserving the marinade, and fry for 30 seconds per side, flipping gently.
6. Add the marinade and fry the fish for 30 more seconds on each side.
7. Garnish with the sesame seeds and scallions and serve on top of the rice.

INGREDIENT TIP: *Genmaicha green tea is a Japanese tea that is made with toasted brown rice, giving it a nutty flavor. Brew a pot of it for the rice, as well as for sipping while you cook.*

SALMON AND OYSTER SAUCE WITH VEGETABLES

SERVES: 4   **PREP TIME:** 15 minutes   **COOK TIME:** 6 minutes

This is a very auspicious dish. Fish and oysters are both positive symbols in China. The word for fish sounds like "abundance" or "prosperity" in Chinese. The word "oyster" in Chinese sounds similar to "good things." In addition, valuable pearls are cultivated in oysters. The Chinese dragon is the keeper of the pearl of wisdom, which, of course, comes from the oyster.

- ½ cup oyster sauce
- 2 tablespoons rice wine
- 1 pound thick, center-cut salmon fillet, cut into 1-inch pieces
- 2 tablespoons cooking oil

- 2 garlic cloves, crushed and chopped
- 1 tablespoon crushed and chopped ginger
- 1 red onion, cut into 1-inch pieces

- 1 red bell pepper, cut into 1-inch pieces
- 2 baby bok choy, leaves separated
- 4 scallions, cut into ½-inch pieces

1. In a large bowl, whisk together the oyster sauce and rice wine. Add the salmon and let marinate while you stir-fry.

2. In a wok over high heat, heat the cooking oil until it shimmers.

3. Add the garlic, ginger, and onion and stir-fry for 1 minute.

4. Add the salmon, reserving the marinade, and gently stir-fry for 1 minute.

5. Add the bell pepper and stir-fry for 1 minute.

6. Add the bok choy and stir-fry for 1 minute.

7. Add the reserved marinade and scallions to the wok and gently stir-fry for 1 minute. Serve over steamed rice.

SHREDDED ROOT VEGETABLES AND SEAFOOD

SERVES: 4   **PREP TIME:** 15 minutes   **COOK TIME:** 6 minutes

For this dish, you may have a good excuse to get a new kitchen tool. A julienne peeler is a vegetable peeler with a serrated blade that cuts thin ribbons or noodles from carrots, squash, parsnips, sweet potatoes, and other firm vegetables. Think of it as a simple spiralizer that makes great vegetables for stir-frying. Of course, you can still julienne with a sharp knife, if you prefer.

- 2 tablespoons cooking oil
- 2 garlic cloves, crushed and chopped
- 1 tablespoon crushed, chopped ginger
- ½ cup julienned carrots
- ½ cup julienned parsnips
- ¼ pound medium shrimp, shelled and deveined
- ½ cup julienned zucchini
- ¼ pound sea scallops, cut in half widthwise
- ¼ pound squid tentacles, rinsed in cold water
- ¼ cup hoisin sauce
- 4 scallions, cut into ½-inch pieces

1. In a wok over high heat, heat the cooking oil until it shimmers.
2. Add the garlic and ginger and stir-fry for 30 seconds.
3. Add the carrots and parsnips and stir-fry for 1 minute.
4. Add the shrimp and stir-fry for 1 minute.
5. Add the zucchini and stir-fry for 30 seconds.
6. Add the scallops and stir-fry for 30 seconds, or until the edges are just cracked.
7. Add the squid and stir-fry for 30 seconds, or until the tentacles are just curled.
8. Add the hoisin sauce and stir-fry for 30 seconds.
9. Garnish with the scallions and serve over steamed rice.

CHANGE IT UP: *You can also julienne turnips, sweet potatoes, beets, and large rainbow radishes for this stir-fry.*

SEAFOOD SALPICAO

SERVES: 4   **PREP TIME:** 15 minutes   **COOK TIME:** 8 minutes

The name of this spicy Filipino dish is derived from the Spanish word for pepper. The combination of sweet oyster sauce and peppery sesame oil reflects the 300-year history and fusion of European and Asian cultures in the Philippines.

- 1 teaspoon hot sesame oil
- 1 tablespoon brown sugar
- ¼ cup oyster sauce
- ¼ cup vegetable or meat broth
- 1 tablespoon cornstarch
- 2 tablespoons cooking oil

- 4 garlic cloves, crushed and chopped
- 1 medium onion, cut into 1-inch pieces
- 4 ounces shiitake mushrooms, sliced
- ¼ pound medium shrimp, shelled and deveined
- 1 cup broccoli florets

- ¼ pound scallops, cut in half widthwise
- 2 cups sugar snap or snow pea pods
- 1 red bell pepper, cut into 1-inch pieces
- ¼ pound squid tentacles, rinsed in cold water

1. In a small bowl, whisk together the sesame oil, brown sugar, oyster sauce, broth, and cornstarch. Set aside.

2. In a wok over high heat, heat the cooking oil until it shimmers.

3. Add the garlic and onion and stir-fry for 1 minute.

4. Add the mushrooms and stir-fry for 1 minute.

5. Add the shrimp and stir-fry for 1 minute.

6. Add the broccoli and stir-fry for 1 minute.

7. Add the scallops and stir-fry for 30 seconds.

8. Add the pea pods and stir-fry for 1 minute.

9. Add the bell pepper and stir-fry for 1 minute.

10. Add the squid and stir-fry for 30 seconds.

11. Add the sesame oil mixture to the wok and stir-fry until a glaze forms. Serve over steamed rice.

HOT AND SOUR SEAFOOD SOUP

SERVES: 4 **PREP TIME:** 15 minutes **COOK TIME:** 8 minutes

This is a hearty pan-Asian soup. You can change up the source of the heat from hot peppers, spicy oils, and fermented chile pastes, and reduce the amounts to suit your taste. The sour can come from a variety of aged rice and wine vinegars or citrus fruits. The key is all in the timing to make sure the seafood is not overcooked.

- 3 quarts vegetable, fish, or meat broth
- 1 tablespoon hot sesame oil
- ¼ cup rice vinegar
- 2 tablespoons cornstarch
- 1 tablespoon cooking oil

- 2 garlic cloves, crushed and chopped
- 1 tablespoon crushed, chopped ginger
- ¼ pound ground pork
- ½ cup julienned carrots
- 1 cup chopped bok choy

- ¼ pound medium shrimp, shelled and deveined
- ¼ pound white fish (like cod or haddock), cut into 1-inch pieces
- ¼ pound sea scallops, cut in half widthwise
- 4 scallions, cut into ½-inch pieces

1. In a large bowl, whisk together the broth, sesame oil, rice vinegar, and cornstarch. Set aside.
2. In a wok over high heat, heat the cooking oil until it shimmers.
3. Add the garlic, ginger, and pork and stir-fry for 1 minute.
4. Add the carrots and stir-fry for 1 minute.
5. Add the broth mixture to the wok and stir until the cornstarch dissolves and the broth comes to a boil.
6. Add the bok choy and let cook for 1 minute.
7. Add the shrimp, followed by the fish and scallops. Cook for 2 minutes.
8. Garnish with the scallions and serve immediately.

Orange Chicken [page 74]

[FIVE]

CHICKEN

CHICKEN

This chapter starts with my favorite chicken stir-fry recipe: Five-Spice Chicken! It is a flavor adaptation of my favorite way to cook chicken, which is roasting it whole in a wok. (A recipe and explanation of why it's a great way to prepare chicken is in my first book, *Easy Chinese Cookbook: Restaurant Favorites Made Simple*.) But roasting a whole chicken can take a couple of hours depending on its size. When I want the licorice-honey glaze of roasted five-spice chicken but don't have the time or a whole chicken ready to roast, stir-fried Five-Spice Chicken is my go-to dish.

While all parts of the chicken (even the feet and head!) are edible, I prefer skinless, boneless thighs when preparing chicken stir-fry. Dark thigh meat has a slightly higher amount of fat than light breast meat, giving it more flavor. Because of the higher fat content, thigh meat also stays moist even when it is cooked well-done. Whether you are using the leaner breast or the more flavorful thigh meat, you will want to slice it into "chopstick-" or bite-size pieces. Also note that cutting it across the grain makes the meat more tender and helps it absorb more flavor when you marinate it.

FIVE-SPICE CHICKEN

SERVES: 4 **PREP TIME:** 15 minutes **COOK TIME:** 6 minutes

This classic Sichuan dish uses five-spice powder, a Chinese-style curry mix. The five spices often ground into this mix are star anise, cinnamon, Sichuan peppercorns, fennel, and cloves. Five-spice powder can be found in the spice or international sections of some supermarkets, in all Asian markets, and online.

- 2 tablespoons soy sauce
- 2 tablespoons rice wine
- ¼ cup honey
- 1 tablespoon Chinese five-spice powder
- 1 pound boneless chicken thighs, cut into 1-inch pieces

- 2 tablespoons cooking oil
- 1 medium carrot, roll-cut into ½-inch pieces
- 1 tablespoon crushed, chopped ginger
- 3 garlic cloves, crushed and chopped
- 1 medium onion, cut into 1-inch pieces

- 1 medium red bell pepper, cut into 1-inch pieces
- 1 tablespoon cornstarch
- 1 teaspoon hot sesame oil
- 4 scallions, cut into 1-inch pieces

1. In a large bowl or resealable plastic bag, mix the soy sauce, rice wine, honey, and five-spice powder. Add the chicken and set aside to marinate.

2. In a wok over high heat, heat the cooking oil until it shimmers.

3. Add the carrot, ginger, and garlic and stir-fry for 1 minute.

4. Add the chicken, reserving the marinade, to the wok and stir-fry for 1 minute.

5. Add the onion and stir-fry for 1 minute.

6. Add the bell pepper and stir-fry for 1 minute.

7. Add the reserved marinade and the cornstarch and stir until a light glaze forms.

8. Add the sesame oil and stir-fry for 30 seconds.

9. Garnish with the scallions. Serve immediately over steamed rice.

PREPARATION TIP: *If you use a resealable plastic bag to marinate the chicken at room temperature, massage the chicken in the marinade to increase the absorption of flavors and moisture before stir-frying it.*

MOO GOO GAI PAN

SERVES: 4   **PREP TIME:** 15 minutes   **COOK TIME:** 6 minutes

The literal translation of this classic Cantonese stir-fry dish is "mushrooms with sliced chicken." Although the name only identifies mushrooms and chicken, there are always other vegetables and a thickened soy-based sauce flavored with the Cantonese trinity of ginger, garlic, and scallions.

- 2 tablespoons soy sauce
- 2 tablespoons rice wine
- 2 tablespoons rice vinegar
- 2 tablespoons sugar
- 1 tablespoon cornstarch
- 2 tablespoons cooking oil

- 1 tablespoon crushed, chopped ginger
- 2 cloves garlic, crushed and chopped
- 1 pound boneless chicken thighs, cut into 1-inch pieces
- 4 ounces sliced mushrooms

- 2 cups sugar snap or snow pea pods
- 1 medium red bell pepper, cut into ½-inch pieces
- 4 scallions, cut into 1-inch pieces

1. In a small bowl, whisk together the soy sauce, rice wine, rice vinegar, sugar, and cornstarch. Set aside.
2. In a wok over high heat, heat the cooking oil until it shimmers.
3. Add the ginger, garlic, and chicken and stir-fry for 1 minute.
4. Add the mushrooms and stir-fry for 1 minute.
5. Add the pea pods and stir-fry for 1 minute.
6. Add the bell pepper and stir-fry for 1 minute.
7. Stir the soy sauce mixture into the wok and stir until a light glaze forms.
8. Garnish with the scallions and serve over steamed rice.

CHANGE IT UP: *You can increase the mushroom flavor by adding dried sliced shiitake mushrooms. They are available at some grocery stores, most Asian markets, and online. You'll need to soak them for 15 minutes in hot water and drain them before adding to the stir-fry.*

SWEET AND SOUR CHICKEN

SERVES: 4   **PREP TIME:** 15 minutes   **COOK TIME:** 8 minutes

Chinese sweet and sour sauce was created in the 1700s in China. It was originally used as a dipping sauce and eventually came to be used as a finishing sauce for stir-fries. A note on using pineapple in your stir-fry: There is a difference between using fresh versus canned pineapple. Fresh pineapple contains an enzyme called bromelain, which is a powerful meat tenderizer. If you marinate meat in fresh pineapple or its juice, it can make the meat more tender, but if you let it sit too long it can make the meat mushy. Heat neutralizes the enzyme, so canned or cooked pineapple will not affect the texture of your meat.

- ¼ cup rice vinegar
- 2 tablespoons ketchup
- 1 (8-ounce) can pineapple chunks, drained, juice reserved
- ¼ cup plus 2 tablespoons cornstarch, divided
- 1 pound boneless chicken thighs, cut into 1-inch pieces
- ¼ cup cooking oil
- 1 tablespoon crushed, chopped ginger
- 2 garlic cloves, crushed and chopped
- 2 cups sugar snap or snow pea pods
- 1 medium red bell pepper, cut into 1-inch pieces
- 4 scallions, cut into 1-inch pieces

1. In a small bowl, whisk together the rice vinegar, ketchup, pineapple juice, and 2 tablespoons of the cornstarch. Set aside.
2. Coat the chicken with the remaining ¼ cup of cornstarch by tossing in a resealable plastic bag or covered bowl. Set aside.
3. Heat the cooking oil in a wok over high heat until it shimmers.
4. Add the ginger and garlic and stir-fry for 30 seconds to lightly brown.
5. Add the chicken and shallow-fry for 3 to 4 minutes until lightly browned.
6. Remove the chicken from the wok and set aside.
7. Remove and discard all but 2 tablespoons of oil from the wok.
8. Add the pea pods and stir-fry for 30 seconds.
9. Add the bell pepper and stir-fry for 30 seconds.

10. Add the pineapple chunks and stir-fry for 30 seconds.

11. Add the rice vinegar mixture and stir until a glaze forms.

12. Return the chicken to the wok, toss with the other ingredients, and garnish with the scallions. Serve with steamed rice.

COOKING TIP: *Think of shallow-frying as a method between stir-frying, where very little oil is used to sear ingredients, and deep-frying, where ingredients are submerged in oil and fried until crispy. With shallow-frying, the ingredients are covered about halfway in oil while sitting in the bottom of the pan. Shallow-frying helps cornstarch or batter stay on the ingredients, as the bottom of the pan will hold it there while frying.*

ORANGE CHICKEN

SERVES: 4 **PREP TIME:** 15 minutes **COOK TIME:** 8 minutes

Orange Chicken is the name of a Chinese-American recipe developed for the Panda Express restaurant chain by chef Andy Kao. It is reminiscent of a Chinese dish known as Dried Orange Peel Chicken. But in order to use the dried orange peel in a stir-fry, you need to rehydrate it first, as dried orange peel is usually intended to flavor marinades. Dried orange peels also include the white pith, which has a bitter, medicinal taste. Unlike the old Chinese version, this recipe uses fresh orange peels.

- Zest of 1 orange
- 1 teaspoon hot sesame oil
- ¼ cup plus 2 tablespoons cornstarch, divided
- ¼ cup orange juice
- 2 tablespoons rice vinegar
- 2 tablespoons rice wine

- 2 tablespoons brown sugar
- 2 tablespoons soy sauce
- 1 pound boneless chicken thighs, cut into 1-inch pieces
- ¼ cup cooking oil
- 1 tablespoon crushed, chopped ginger

- 2 garlic cloves, crushed and chopped
- 1 medium onion, cut into 1-inch pieces
- 2 cups sugar snap or snow pea pods
- 1 medium red bell pepper, cut into 1-inch pieces
- 4 scallions, cut into 1-inch pieces

1. In a small bowl, whisk together the orange zest, sesame oil, 2 tablespoons of the cornstarch, the orange juice, rice vinegar, rice wine, brown sugar, and soy sauce. Set aside.

2. Coat the chicken with the remaining ¼ cup of cornstarch by tossing in a resealable plastic bag or covered bowl, ensuring the pieces are evenly coated.

3. In a wok over high heat, heat the cooking oil until it shimmers.

4. Add the ginger and garlic and stir-fry for 30 seconds.

5. Shallow-fry (see page 73) the chicken for 3 to 4 minutes until lightly browned.

6. Remove the chicken and set aside. Remove and discard all but 2 tablespoons of oil from the wok.

7. Add the onion to the wok and stir-fry for 1 minute.

8. Add the pea pods and stir-fry for 30 seconds.

9. Add the bell pepper and stir-fry for 30 seconds.

10. Add the orange juice mixture and stir until a glaze forms.

11. Return the chicken to the wok. Toss, garnish with the scallions, and serve over rice.

CHANGE IT UP: *If you have a blender or food processor, you can replace the orange juice and sugar with ¼ cup of pureed orange.*

COCONUT CHICKEN

SERVES: 4   **PREP TIME:** 15 minutes   **COOK TIME:** 6 minutes

This effortless Thai chicken stir-fry dish features a dynamic duo of sweet coconut and pungent fish sauce that will be sure to satisfy a variety of palates. Hot sesame oil stars in a spicy finish. Eat this if you want to wake up your taste buds!

- ¼ cup canned coconut milk
- 2 tablespoons fish sauce
- 2 tablespoons lime juice
- 1 teaspoon hot sesame oil
- 1 tablespoon cornstarch

- 2 tablespoons coconut oil
- 1 tablespoon crushed, chopped ginger
- 2 garlic cloves, crushed and chopped
- 1 pound boneless chicken thighs, cut into 1-inch pieces

- 1 medium red onion, cut into 1-inch pieces
- 2 cups sugar snap or snow pea pods
- ½ cup chopped cilantro or parsley

1. In a small bowl, whisk together the coconut milk, fish sauce, lime juice, sesame oil, and cornstarch. Set aside.

2. In a wok over high heat, heat the coconut oil until it shimmers.

3. Add the ginger, garlic, and chicken and stir-fry for 1 minute.

4. Add the onion and stir-fry for 1 minute.

5. Add the pea pods and stir-fry for 1 minute.

6. Add the coconut milk mixture to the wok and stir until a glaze forms.

7. Garnish with the chopped cilantro or parsley and serve over coconut steamed jasmine rice.

CILANTRO-LIME CHICKEN

SERVES: 4 | **PREP TIME:** 15 minutes | **COOK TIME:** 6 minutes

This recipe uses a fair amount of cilantro. Some people love it, but other folks can't stand it because they think it tastes like soap. And they're not exactly wrong—cilantro contains an enzyme that's very closely related to chemicals found in soap. Some people have a gene that causes them to be more sensitive to that enzyme. Cilantro is also known as coriander, Chinese parsley, and Thai parsley. In place of cilantro, you can use parsley, which has a milder flavor.

- 1 (8-ounce) can of pineapple chunks, drained, juice reserved
- Zest and juice of 1 lime
- 2 tablespoons fish sauce
- 1 tablespoon cornstarch
- 2 tablespoons cooking oil
- 1 tablespoon crushed, chopped ginger
- 2 garlic cloves, crushed and chopped
- 1 pound boneless chicken thighs, cut into 1-inch pieces
- 1 medium onion, cut into 1-inch pieces
- 2 cups sugar snap or snow pea pods
- 1 medium red bell pepper, cut into 1-inch pieces
- 1 cup chopped cilantro

1. In a small bowl, whisk together the pineapple juice, lime zest and juice, fish sauce, and cornstarch. Set aside.
2. In a wok over high heat, heat the cooking oil until it shimmers.
3. Add the ginger, garlic, and chicken and stir-fry for 1 minute.
4. Add the onion and stir-fry for 1 minute.
5. Add the pea pods and stir-fry for 1 minute.
6. Add the bell pepper and stir-fry for 1 minute.
7. Add the pineapple chunks to the wok and stir-fry for 1 minute.
8. Add the pineapple and lime juice mixture to the wok and stir until a light glaze is formed.
9. Garnish with the cilantro and serve over jasmine rice.

CHANGE IT UP: *Serve with sliced lime wedges on the side for a fresh citrus kick.*

LEMONGRASS CHICKEN

SERVES: 4　　　　**PREP TIME:** 15 minutes　　　**COOK TIME:** 6 minutes

Lemongrass is a tropical grass commonly grown in Southeast Asia and is used either fresh or dried in cooking to impart a lemony flavor. This recipe calls for fresh lemongrass, which is available at some grocery stores and most Asian markets.

- 2 tablespoons cooking oil
- 1 tablespoon crushed, chopped ginger
- 2 garlic cloves, crushed and chopped
- 2 lemongrass hearts (the bottom 2 inches of the white inner layers), finely minced
- 1 pound boneless chicken thighs, cut into 1-inch pieces
- 1 medium red onion, cut into 1-inch pieces
- 4 ounces sliced mushrooms
- 1 medium red bell pepper, cut into 1-inch pieces
- 2 heads baby bok choy, leaves separated
- 1 teaspoon fish sauce
- 1 teaspoon hot sesame oil
- Fresh chopped herbs, such as cilantro, mint, or parsley, for garnish

1. In a wok over high heat, heat the cooking oil until it shimmers.
2. Add the ginger, garlic, lemongrass, and chicken and stir-fry for 1 minute.
3. Add the onion and stir-fry for 1 minute.
4. Add the mushrooms and stir-fry for 1 minute.
5. Add the bell pepper and stir-fry for 1 minute.
6. Add the bok choy, fish sauce, and sesame oil and stir-fry for 30 seconds.
7. Garnish with chopped herbs of your choice and serve over steamed rice.

INGREDIENT TIP: *The outer leaves and stalks of store-bought lemongrass will need to be peeled off to get to the soft white hearts. You can use the dried outer parts for flavor in cooking and making tea, but they will need to be removed before stir-frying, as they are too tough to eat.*

GROUND CHICKEN AND VEGETABLES WITH HOISIN SAUCE

SERVES: 4   PREP TIME: 10 minutes   COOK TIME: 5 minutes

Hoisin sauce is a thick, umami-rich sauce made from fermented soybeans, peppers, fennel, garlic, and sugar. It is most closely associated with Cantonese recipes, but its use has spread all over Asia and beyond. In Chinese cooking, hoisin sauce is vegetarian and is like oyster sauce, but without any seafood.

- 2 tablespoons cooking oil
- 1 tablespoon crushed, chopped ginger
- 2 garlic cloves, crushed and chopped
- 1 medium carrot, roll-cut into ½-inch pieces
- 1 pound ground chicken
- 1 medium onion, cut into 1-inch pieces
- 2 cups sugar snap or snow pea pods
- ¼ cup hoisin sauce

1. In a wok over high heat, heat the cooking oil until it shimmers.
2. Add the ginger, garlic, carrot, and chicken and stir-fry for 1 minute.
3. Add the onion and stir-fry for 1 minute.
4. Add the pea pods and stir-fry for 1 minute.
5. Add the hoisin sauce and stir-fry for 30 seconds.
6. Serve over steamed rice.

CHANGE IT UP: *Substituting oyster sauce or your favorite barbecue sauce for the hoisin sauce will give you and your family some variety. Just remember to add the sauce at the end of your stir-fry.*

KADAI CHICKEN

SERVES: 4   **PREP TIME:** 15 minutes   **COOK TIME:** 8 minutes

This quick Indian-inspired chicken stir-fry uses a combination of curry spices for flavor, hot peppers for heat, and yogurt for creaminess. The word curry is actually an English word taken from the Tamil word kari, meaning sauce.

- 2 tablespoons ghee (see Preparation Tip)
- 1 tablespoon crushed, chopped ginger
- 2 garlic cloves, crushed and chopped
- 1 medium carrot, roll-cut into ½-inch pieces
- 1 pound boneless chicken thighs, cut into 1-inch pieces
- 1 medium onion, cut into 1-inch pieces
- 1 teaspoon ground coriander
- 1 teaspoon cumin
- 1 teaspoon paprika
- 2 chiles, sliced into ¼-inch circles (no need to core or seed them)
- ½ cup whole-milk Greek yogurt

1. In a wok over high heat, heat the ghee until it shimmers.
2. Add the ginger, garlic, carrot, and chicken and stir-fry for 1 minute.
3. Add the onion, coriander, cumin, and paprika and stir-fry for 1 minute.
4. Add the sliced chiles and stir-fry for 1 minute.
5. Turn off the heat and stir the yogurt into the wok. Serve over basmati rice.

PREPARATION TIP: *You can make your own ghee (clarified butter) by melting butter, letting it cool, then skimming off the milk solids that float to the top. The butter that remains is ghee. Milk solids burn at a lower temperature and impact flavor when used as a stir-fry cooking oil at high temperatures. If you wish, feel free to add the milk solids back into the stir-fry at the end of the cooking process.*

KIMCHI CHICKEN AND CABBAGE

SERVES: 4   **PREP TIME:** 10 minutes   **COOK TIME:** 5 minutes

This stir-fry needs very little preparation and still comes out delicious. The ground chicken absorbs all the sumptuous flavors of the kimchi, fish sauce, and gochujang chili sauce, resulting in an incredibly tasty dish. Make sure your rice is ready to go, as you'll want to plate and eat this hearty dish as soon as it's finished cooking.

- 2 tablespoons cooking oil
- 1 tablespoon crushed, chopped ginger
- 2 garlic cloves, crushed and chopped
- 1 pound ground chicken
- 1 cup chopped kimchi
- 2 heads baby bok choy, leaves separated
- 1 tablespoon fish sauce
- 1 tablespoon gochujang
- 1 tablespoon toasted sesame oil
- 2 tablespoons sesame seeds

1. In a wok over high heat, heat the cooking oil until it shimmers.

2. Add the ginger, garlic, and chicken and stir-fry for 1 minute.

3. Add the kimchi, bok choy, fish sauce, and gochujang and stir-fry for 1 minute.

4. Add the sesame oil and sesame seeds and toss.

5. Serve over steamed rice.

CASHEW CHICKEN

SERVES: 4   **PREP TIME:** 15 minutes   **COOK TIME:** 8 minutes

Cashew Chicken was invented in 1963 by David Leong, a Chinese-American restaurateur from Springfield, Missouri. His restaurant, Leong's Tea House, served Cantonese fare but wasn't bringing in enough customers. Cashew Chicken was his way of blending Cantonese flavors with Ozark cuisine. His Springfield-style Cashew Chicken was a culinary hit and is now a takeout staple all over the United States.

- 2 tablespoons cooking oil
- 1 tablespoon crushed, chopped ginger
- 2 garlic cloves, crushed and chopped
- 1 medium carrot, roll-cut into ½-inch pieces

- 1 pound boneless chicken thighs, cut into 1-inch pieces
- 1 medium onion, cut into 1-inch pieces
- 4 ounces sliced mushrooms
- 1 red bell pepper, cut into 1-inch pieces

- 2 cups sugar snap or snow pea pods
- ½ cup whole cashews
- ¼ cup oyster sauce
- 2 tablespoons soy sauce
- 4 scallions, cut into 1-inch pieces

1. In a wok over high heat, heat the cooking oil until it shimmers.
2. Add the ginger, garlic, and carrot and stir-fry for 1 minute.
3. Add the chicken and onion and stir-fry for 1 minute.
4. Add the mushrooms and bell pepper and stir-fry for 1 minute.
5. Add the pea pods and cashews and stir-fry for 1 minute.
6. Add the oyster sauce and soy sauce and stir-fry for 1 minute.
7. Garnish with the scallions and serve over steamed rice.

INGREDIENT TIP: *The Leongs use asparagus and broccolini as well as other locally available vegetables in their signature dish. Feel free to change up the vegetables and use whatever you like.*

HONEY-GARLIC CHICKEN

SERVES: 4   **PREP TIME:** 15 minutes   **COOK TIME:** 6 minutes

Lightly browned garlic and a honey glaze—what's not to like? This classic Cantonese-style dish is a crowd-pleaser you'll want to make again and again.

- 2 tablespoons soy sauce
- 2 tablespoons honey
- 1 tablespoon cornstarch
- 2 tablespoons cooking oil
- 1 tablespoon crushed, chopped ginger
- 3 garlic cloves, crushed and chopped
- 1 medium carrot, roll-cut into ½-inch pieces
- 1 pound boneless chicken thighs, cut into 1-inch pieces
- 1 medium onion, cut into 1-inch pieces
- 1 cup broccoli florets, cut into bite-size pieces
- 1 red bell pepper, cut into 1-inch pieces
- 4 scallions, cut into 1-inch pieces

1. In a small bowl, whisk together the soy sauce, honey, and cornstarch. Set aside.
2. In a wok over high heat, heat the cooking oil until it shimmers.
3. Add the ginger, garlic, carrot, and chicken and stir-fry for 1 minute.
4. Add the onion and stir-fry for 1 minute.
5. Add the broccoli and stir-fry for 1 minute.
6. Add the bell pepper and stir-fry for 1 minute.
7. Add soy sauce mixture to the wok and stir until a glaze forms.
8. Garnish with the scallions and serve over steamed rice.

CHANGE IT UP: *This recipe is mild enough that the flavors of other vegetables can come through very easily. Mild Chinese cabbages such as bok choy and napa work well when added near the end so they stay crunchy.*

BUTTER CHICKEN

SERVES: 4   **PREP TIME:** 15 minutes   **COOK TIME:** 6 minutes

This recipe is an adaptation of a very popular dish created in 1947 by the founders of the Moti Mahal restaurant in Delhi, India. The story goes that Butter Chicken was invented by mistake when the owner of the restaurant decided to rejuvenate some dried-up pieces of unsold tandoori chicken by soaking them in a gravy made from curry, butter, and cream. After some time, the chicken became very tender and flavorful. The newly discovered dish made Moti Mahal famous and spread around the world from there. In this adaptation, we quickly stir-fry the chicken in butter and spices before creating a creamy sauce with yogurt. For the best flavor, be sure to use whole-milk Greek yogurt.

- 2 tablespoons ghee
- 1 tablespoon crushed, chopped ginger
- 2 garlic cloves, crushed and chopped
- 1 medium carrot, roll-cut into ½-inch pieces
- 1 pound boneless chicken thighs, cut into 1-inch pieces
- 1 medium onion, cut into 1-inch pieces
- 1 red bell pepper, cut into 1-inch pieces
- 1 teaspoon ground cumin
- 1 teaspoon ground coriander
- 1 teaspoon ground paprika
- 1 teaspoon ground cloves
- 2 tablespoons salted butter
- 1 teaspoon hot sesame oil
- ½ cup whole-milk Greek yogurt

1. In a wok over high heat, heat the ghee until it shimmers.
2. Add the ginger, garlic, and carrot and stir-fry for 1 minute.
3. Add the chicken, onion, bell pepper, cumin, coriander, paprika, and cloves and stir-fry for 1 minute.
4. Add the butter and sesame oil and stir-fry for 1 minute.
5. Turn off the heat and stir in the yogurt.
6. Serve over basmati rice.

MALAYSIAN CHICKEN

SERVES: 4   **PREP TIME:** 15 minutes   **COOK TIME:** 6 minutes

Sambal oelek, a Malaysian chili paste, gives sriracha a run for its money in terms of heat. "Sambal" refers to a sauce made of hot peppers, and "oelek" refers to the mortar and pestle used to prepare the sauce. Because sambal oelek has less vinegar than sriracha, you can add heat without impacting the taste of a dish. A little goes a long way, so if you're a newbie to the spice world, start slow! Sambal oelek can be found in the international sections of many grocery stores or at Asian markets, but if you can't find it, substitute with sriracha in the same amount.

- 2 tablespoons cooking oil
- 1 tablespoon crushed, chopped ginger
- 2 garlic cloves, crushed and chopped
- 1 pound boneless chicken thighs, cut into 1-inch pieces
- 1 medium red onion, cut into 1-inch pieces
- ¼ cup sambal oelek
- 1 tablespoon fish sauce
- 1 cup chopped bok choy
- 4 scallions, cut into 1-inch pieces

1. In a wok over high heat, heat the cooking oil until it shimmers.
2. Add the ginger, garlic, and chicken and stir-fry for 1 minute.
3. Add the onion and stir-fry for 1 minute.
4. Add the sambal oelek and stir-fry for 30 seconds.
5. Add the fish sauce and bok choy and stir-fry for 1 minute.
6. Garnish with the scallions and serve over jasmine rice.

CHANGE IT UP: *If you use ground chicken or turkey instead of chopped chicken thighs, this stir-fry will cook even faster. Plus, the sambal oelek and fish sauce will nicely coat and infuse the ground meat with flavor.*

CHICKEN STIR-FRY SOUP

SERVES: 4   **PREP TIME:** 15 minutes   **COOK TIME:** 6 minutes

Chicken soup makes us feel better when we're sick and is a delicious meal at any time, so how about a version that comes together almost instantly? The stir-fry version of this quintessential comfort food has immunity-boosting ginger, healthy veggies, and fresh herbs that are sure to get you back on your feet in no time.

- 2 tablespoons cooking oil
- 1 tablespoon crushed, chopped ginger
- 2 garlic cloves, crushed and chopped
- 1 pound ground or finely chopped chicken

- 1 medium onion, diced
- 1 bell pepper (any color), cut into ½-inch pieces
- 1 cup chopped bok choy
- 3 quarts meat or vegetable broth

- 4 scallions, cut into ¼-inch pieces
- Fresh chopped herbs such as cilantro, mint, parsley, or basil, for garnish

1. In a wok over high heat, heat the cooking oil until it shimmers.
2. Add the ginger, garlic, chicken, onion, and bell pepper and stir-fry for 1 minute.
3. Add the bok choy and stir-fry for 30 seconds.
4. Add the broth and bring to a gentle boil.
5. Add the scallions, squeezing them to bruise while sprinkling them into the soup.
6. Serve the soup topped with chopped herbs.

CHANGE IT UP: *Add some hot sesame oil if you really want to clear your sinuses.*

Chili Pork and Eggplant [page 99]

PORK

PORK

Pork has long played an important role in Chinese culture. Pigs were domesticated in China over 10,000 years ago and have since taken on profound symbolism for the Chinese people as tokens of prosperity and good luck. Additionally, people born in the lunar year of the pig are said to be good-tempered, kind, positive, and loyal. Indeed, even the pictograph for "home" in Chinese is a roof with a pig underneath. The sumptuous flavors of pork also play a large role in many Asian dishes, from spareribs to pork fried rice. Now, pork is the most widely consumed meat in Asia and around the world.

When choosing the right cut of pork for stir-frying, there are two good options. My first choice is pork butt because it is evenly marbled with fat, which gives it more flavor and juiciness than other cuts. Interestingly, pork butt is not from the back of the pig, but rather from the upper front shoulder. Pork tenderloin is also a good stir-fry choice. It is leaner but more tender. Try both and then decide which you prefer.

SWEET AND SOUR PORK

SERVES: 4   **PREP TIME:** 15 minutes   **COOK TIME:** 6 minutes

This famous Cantonese dish from southern China was originally made with pork ribs. It's been said that foreigners visiting Guangdong loved the sweet and sour sauce but complained about having to deal with the bones. The local chefs switched to boneless pork but kept the same sauce, creating the dish we know today.

- 1 (8-ounce) can pineapple chunks, drained, juice reserved
- ¼ cup rice vinegar
- ¼ cup plus 2 tablespoons cornstarch, divided
- 2 tablespoons brown sugar
- 1 pound pork tenderloin, cut into 1-inch pieces
- ¼ cup cooking oil
- 1 tablespoon crushed, chopped ginger
- 2 garlic cloves, crushed and chopped
- 1 medium red onion, cut into 1-inch pieces
- 1 red bell pepper, cut into 1-inch pieces
- 4 scallions, cut into 1-inch pieces

1. In a small bowl, whisk together the reserved pineapple juice, rice vinegar, 2 tablespoons of the cornstarch, and brown sugar. Set aside.

2. Add the pork to a resealable plastic bag or covered bowl. Toss with the remaining ¼ cup of cornstarch to coat completely.

3. In a wok over high heat, heat the cooking oil until it shimmers.

4. Add the ginger and garlic and stir-fry for 1 minute.

5. Add the pork and shallow-fry (see page 73) until lightly browned. Remove the pork and set aside.

6. Remove and discard all but 2 tablespoons of oil from the wok.

7. Add the onion to the wok and stir-fry for 1 minute.

8. Add the bell pepper and pineapple chunks and stir-fry for 1 minute.

9. Add the pineapple juice mixture and stir until a glaze forms. Stir in the cooked pork.

10. Garnish with the scallions and serve over steamed rice.

CHANGE IT UP: *If you don't like pineapple, try this dish with other types of canned fruit like mango or peach mixed with citrus juice for acidity.*

SESAME PORK

SERVES: 4   PREP TIME: 15 minutes   COOK TIME: 8 minutes

Sesame seeds have been used in cooking since 3,000 BC. Sesame oil was one of the first edible oils to be pressed for consumption, and the seeds were one of the first condiments used to add crunchiness to a dish. This stir-fry uses both the oil and the seeds to impart a deep, nutty flavor to the dish. When you're eating sesame, you really are enjoying an important aspect of culinary history!

- 2 tablespoons cooking oil
- 1 tablespoon crushed, chopped ginger
- 2 garlic cloves, crushed and chopped
- 1 medium carrot, roll-cut into ½-inch pieces
- 1 pound pork tenderloin, cut into 1-inch pieces
- 1 medium onion, cut into 1-inch pieces
- 1 medium red bell pepper, cut into 1-inch pieces
- 1 teaspoon hot sesame oil
- 2 tablespoons soy sauce
- 2 tablespoons honey
- 1 tablespoon cornstarch
- 2 tablespoons sesame seeds
- 4 scallions, cut into 1-inch pieces

1. In a wok over high heat, heat the cooking oil until it shimmers.
2. Add the ginger, garlic, and carrot and stir-fry for 1 minute.
3. Add the pork and stir-fry for 1 minute.
4. Add the onion and bell pepper and stir-fry for 1 minute.
5. Add the sesame oil, soy sauce, honey, and cornstarch and stir until a light glaze forms.
6. Sprinkle with the sesame seeds, garnish with the scallions, and serve over steamed rice.

CHANGE IT UP: *If you can't find pork tenderloin, you can use pork shoulder. Although it's not as tender as tenderloin, it has more marbling, so it will have a stronger flavor and stay moister.*

KOREAN GINGER-GARLIC PORK

SERVES: 4   **PREP TIME:** 15 minutes   **COOK TIME:** 6 minutes

Gochujang is considered the spicy-sweet-salty miso of Korean cooking. The heft of this sauce is great for pork, and its sweet undertones complement those of the garlic perfectly. Note that gochujang isn't a finishing sauce like sriracha, but rather better to use while cooking. A little goes a long way!

- ½ cup kimchi, cut into ½-inch pieces, drained and juice reserved
- 2 tablespoons rice wine
- ¼ cup gochujang
- 1 tablespoon cornstarch
- 2 tablespoons cooking oil
- 1 tablespoon crushed, chopped ginger
- 2 garlic cloves, crushed and chopped
- 1 pound pork tenderloin, cut into 1-inch pieces
- 4 scallions, cut into 1-inch pieces

1. In a small bowl, whisk together the kimchi juice, rice wine, gochujang, and cornstarch. Set aside.
2. In a wok over high heat, heat the cooking oil until it shimmers.
3. Add the ginger, garlic, and pork and stir-fry for 1 minute.
4. Add the kimchi and stir-fry for 30 seconds.
5. Add the gochujang mixture and stir until a glaze forms.
6. Garnish with the scallions and serve over steamed rice.

FIVE-SPICE PORK WITH BOK CHOY

SERVES: 4   **PREP TIME:** 15 minutes   **COOK TIME:** 6 minutes

Don't be intimidated by a seasoning with five spices. It's meant to include all the tastes: salty, sweet, sour, bitter, and spicy. The complexity of five-spice powder is excellent for savory meat dishes—but it can even be used in baking for an unexpected and warming taste. Here, oyster sauce provides an extra boost of umami and seals in all the flavors with a light glaze.

- 2 tablespoons cooking oil
- 1 tablespoon crushed, chopped ginger
- 2 garlic cloves, crushed and chopped
- 1 pound ground pork
- 1 tablespoon Chinese five-spice powder
- 1 teaspoon hot sesame oil
- 2 cups chopped bok choy
- ¼ cup oyster sauce
- 4 scallions, cut into 1-inch pieces

1. In a wok over high heat, heat the cooking oil until it shimmers.
2. Add the ginger, garlic, pork, and five-spice powder and stir-fry for 1 minute.
3. Add the sesame oil and bok choy and stir-fry for 1 minute.
4. Add the oyster sauce, toss with the stir-fry, and cook for 30 seconds.
5. Garnish with the scallions and serve over steamed rice.

PINEAPPLE PORK AND PEPPERS

SERVES: 4   **PREP TIME:** 15 minutes   **COOK TIME:** 8 minutes

If you're craving something sweeter for dinner, the pineapple in this stir-fry will surely satisfy. Pork and pineapple are a surprising but welcome match made in stir-fry heaven. The rice vinegar works in concert with the spiciness of the peppers by producing a pleasant heat to go with the sweetness of the pineapple.

- 1 (8-ounce) can pineapple chunks, drained, juice reserved
- ¼ cup rice vinegar
- 2 tablespoons brown sugar
- 2 tablespoons cornstarch
- 2 tablespoons cooking oil
- 1 tablespoon crushed, chopped ginger
- 2 garlic cloves, crushed and chopped
- 1 pound pork tenderloin, cut into 1-inch pieces
- 2 chiles, cut into ¼-inch circles (no need to remove seeds or core)
- 1 medium onion, cut into 1-inch pieces
- 1 teaspoon hot sesame oil
- 4 scallions, cut into 1-inch pieces

1. In a small bowl, whisk together the pineapple juice, rice vinegar, brown sugar, and cornstarch. Set aside.
2. In a wok over high heat, heat the cooking oil until it shimmers.
3. Add the ginger, garlic, and pork and stir-fry for 1 minute.
4. Add the chiles and onion and stir-fry for 1 minute.
5. Add the pineapple chunks and sesame oil and stir-fry for 30 seconds.
6. Add the pineapple juice mixture and stir until a glaze forms.
7. Garnish with the scallions and serve over steamed rice.

INGREDIENT TIP: *You can adjust the spiciness by increasing or decreasing the amount of hot sesame oil, as well as by using milder or hotter peppers. Most grocery stores have a heat comparison chart for peppers they sell.*

HOISIN PORK AND MUSHROOMS

SERVES: 4   **PREP TIME:** 15 minutes   **COOK TIME:** 8 minutes

Hoisin sauce is often referred to as Chinese ketchup and is an incredibly versatile condiment. Hoisin goes well with fatty meats like pork and provides a delicious glaze in stir-fry dishes. There are variations between regions and among brands, so taste-test different types of hoisin to see what you like best (you can always use up leftover sauces in marinades).

- 2 tablespoons cooking oil
- 1 tablespoon crushed, chopped ginger
- 2 garlic cloves, crushed and chopped
- 1 pound pork tenderloin, cut into 1-inch pieces
- 1 medium onion, cut into 1-inch pieces
- 4 ounces sliced mushrooms
- 2 cups sugar snap or snow pea pods
- ¼ cup hoisin sauce
- 2 tablespoons soy sauce
- 4 scallions, cut into 1-inch pieces

1. In a wok over high heat, heat the cooking oil until it shimmers.
2. Add the ginger, garlic, and pork and stir-fry for 1 minute.
3. Add the onion and mushrooms and stir-fry for 1 minute.
4. Add the pea pods and stir-fry for 1 minute.
5. Add the hoisin sauce and soy sauce and stir-fry for 30 seconds.
6. Garnish with the scallions and serve over steamed rice.

INGREDIENT TIP: *My go-to brand of hoisin sauce is Lee Kum Kee. It's available in some grocery stores in the international section, in most Asian markets, and online.*

CHILI PORK AND EGGPLANT

SERVES: 4   **PREP TIME:** 15 minutes   **COOK TIME:** 6 minutes

Stir-frying is the best way to cook eggplant. You're not adding any extra moisture, so it won't get soggy. The fats from the oil and the ground pork help the mild-flavored eggplant caramelize and absorb the ginger and garlic aromatics, as well as the hot and sweet glaze of the sriracha and hoisin sauce. Yum!

- 2 tablespoons cooking oil
- 1 tablespoon crushed, chopped ginger
- 2 garlic cloves, crushed and chopped
- 1 small eggplant, diced into ½-inch cubes
- 1 pound ground pork
- 2 chiles, cut into ¼-inch circles (no need to core or seed)
- ¼ cup sriracha
- 2 tablespoons hoisin sauce
- 4 scallions, cut into 1-inch pieces

1. In a wok over high heat, heat the cooking oil until it shimmers.
2. Add the ginger, garlic, and eggplant and stir-fry for 1 minute.
3. Add the pork and stir-fry for 1 minute.
4. Add the chiles, sriracha, and hoisin sauce and stir-fry for 1 minute.
5. Garnish with the scallions and serve over steamed rice.

INGREDIENT TIP: *Chinese eggplants are long and have fewer seeds and thinner skin than Western eggplants. Asian markets have them, as well as many grocery stores. If you are using a globe eggplant instead, look for a small one.*

VIETNAMESE CARAMELIZED PORK

SERVES: 4   **PREP TIME:** 15 minutes   **COOK TIME:** 5 minutes

This sweet, spicy, and salty stir-fry dish is traditionally prepared on the eve of Tet, the Vietnamese New Year, because you're not supposed to cook on New Year's Day. Beginning with New Year's Day and continuing for three days, Vietnamese families focus on honoring the Kitchen God and ancestors, and visiting family members, so almost all the food preparation takes place before New Year's Day. The caramelization coats and seals the pork, keeping it moist when it is heated up the next day (in case you want to celebrate, too).

- 2 tablespoons coconut oil
- 1 tablespoon crushed, chopped ginger
- 2 garlic cloves, crushed and chopped
- 1 medium onion, diced
- 1 pound ground pork
- 1 teaspoon ground black pepper
- 1 tablespoon fish sauce
- ¼ cup brown sugar
- ½ cup chopped kimchi
- 4 scallions, cut into ½-inch pieces

1. In a wok over high heat, heat the coconut oil until it shimmers.
2. Add the ginger, garlic, onion, and pork and stir-fry for 1 minute.
3. Add the black pepper, fish sauce, and brown sugar and stir-fry for 1 minute.
4. Add the kimchi and stir-fry for 30 seconds.
5. Garnish with the scallions and serve over steamed rice cooked in coconut water.

CHANGE IT UP: *You can create your own version of this stir-fry by substituting other ground meats such as beef, lamb, or chicken. Feel free to change up the vegetables as well; just keep in mind that you want to put the ingredients that take the longest to cook into the wok first.*

GROUND PORK AND TOFU WITH GARLIC AND GINGER

SERVES: 4   **PREP TIME: 15 minutes**   **COOK TIME: 6 minutes**

This dish is a simple way to combine the healthy protein of tofu with the pungent flavors of ginger and garlic. The fat from the ground pork helps carry the sweetness of the vegetables and sauce into the stir-fried tofu.

- 2 tablespoons soy sauce
- 2 tablespoons rice wine
- 1 tablespoon cornstarch
- 2 tablespoons cooking oil
- ½ pound extra-firm tofu, cut into 1-inch cubes
- 1 medium carrot, roll-cut into ½-inch pieces
- 1 tablespoon crushed, chopped ginger
- 4 garlic cloves, crushed and chopped
- ½ pound ground pork
- 1 medium onion, cut into 1-inch pieces
- 1 teaspoon Chinese five-spice powder
- 1 medium red bell pepper, cut into 1-inch pieces
- 4 scallions, cut into 1-inch pieces

1. In a small bowl, whisk together the soy sauce, rice wine, and cornstarch. Set aside.
2. In a wok over high heat, heat the cooking oil until it shimmers.
3. Add the tofu, carrot, ginger, and garlic and stir-fry for 2 minutes.
4. Add the pork, onion, and five-spice powder and stir-fry for 1 minute.
5. Add the bell pepper and stir-fry for 1 minute.
6. Add the soy sauce mixture and stir until a glaze forms.
7. Garnish with the scallions and serve over steamed rice.

PREPARATION TIP: *Be sure to drain and pat the tofu dry before stir-frying; it won't cook properly if it's too wet, and patting it dry will reduce splatter when it's placed in the hot oil.*

GROUND PORK AND BRUSSELS SPROUTS WITH OYSTER SAUCE

SERVES: 4   **PREP TIME:** 15 minutes   **COOK TIME:** 5 minutes

Although Brussels sprouts are not native to Asian cooking, their cabbage and mustard green relatives, bok choy and napa from the Brassica family of vegetables, are common in stir-fry. Brussels sprouts are great in stir-fry because their tightly packed heads are perfect for searing and caramelizing their natural sugars without getting soggy.

- 2 tablespoons cooking oil
- 1 tablespoon crushed, chopped ginger
- 2 garlic cloves, crushed and chopped
- 1 dozen Brussels sprouts, trimmed and halved
- 1 medium onion, diced
- 1 pound ground pork
- ¼ cup honey
- ¼ cup oyster sauce

1. In a wok over high heat, heat the cooking oil until it shimmers.
2. Add the ginger, garlic, and Brussels sprouts and stir-fry for 1 minute.
3. Add the onion and pork and stir-fry for 1 minute.
4. Add the honey and stir-fry for 1 minute.
5. Add the oyster sauce and toss for 30 seconds.
6. Serve over steamed rice.

INGREDIENT TIP: *Prepare Brussels sprouts for stir-frying by cutting off any stems and slicing the sprouts in half. Remove any yellow or discolored leaves before searing the sprouts in oil and aromatics near the beginning of the stir-frying process. Leave them in the wok as ingredients are added to continue searing and softening up.*

JAPANESE GINGER PORK (SHOGAYAKI)

SERVES: 4   PREP TIME: 6 minutes   COOK TIME: 4 minutes

There's nothing fancy about this side dish except the taste. Mirin and sake are both Japanese rice wines; mirin is a very sweet, thick wine used only for cooking, while sake (pronounced sah-ke) is used for both cooking and drinking. When used in a recipe, drier sake will lend less sweetness but will serve to tenderize meat. Mirin has less alcohol, so it will make the meat firmer and add sweetness to the recipe.

- 1 tablespoon white miso
- 2 tablespoons tamari
- 2 tablespoons cooking oil
- 2 tablespoons crushed, chopped ginger
- 2 garlic cloves, crushed and chopped
- 1 pound pork tenderloin, cut into 1-inch pieces
- 2 tablespoons sake
- 2 tablespoons mirin
- 2 tablespoons brown sugar

1. In a small bowl, whisk together the miso and tamari. Set aside.
2. In a wok over high heat, heat the cooking oil until it shimmers.
3. Add the ginger, garlic, pork, and sake and stir-fry for 1 minute.
4. Add the mirin and brown sugar and stir-fry for 1 minute.
5. Stir in the miso and tamari mixture and toss.
6. Serve the pork over sushi rice.

INGREDIENT TIP: *Sushi rice made with green genmaicha tea goes great with this simple side dish.*

MYANMARESE RED PORK BOWL

SERVES: 4   **PREP TIME:** 15 minutes   **COOK TIME:** 8 minutes

The main ingredient in the original version of this recipe is the famous Chinese ham from Jinhua, China. Jinhua hams have been produced continuously for over 1,200 years. There are references to their quality and taste in Marco Polo's letters. Jinhua hams cannot be imported to the United States because they do not follow US standards for ham production. For the closest flavor, you'll want to buy the authentic Smithfield ham, as it has been cured the longest and will have the deepest smoked flavor. An interesting side note: Smithfield Ham was purchased by a Chinese pork company in 2013.

- ¼ cup rice wine
- 1 tablespoon cornstarch
- 2 tablespoons brown sugar
- 2 tablespoons cooking oil
- 1 tablespoon crushed, chopped ginger
- 2 garlic cloves, crushed and chopped
- ½ pound Smithfield ham, cut into ½-inch pieces
- 2 chiles, cut into ¼-inch circles (no need to core or seed)
- 1 teaspoon hot sesame oil
- 2 tablespoons soy sauce
- ¼ cup sriracha
- 4 scallions, cut into ½-inch pieces
- Fresh chopped cilantro, for garnish

1. In a small bowl, whisk together the rice wine, cornstarch, and brown sugar. Set aside.
2. In a wok over high heat, heat the cooking oil until it shimmers.
3. Add the ginger, garlic, and ham and stir-fry for 1 minute.
4. Add the chiles, sesame oil, soy sauce, and sriracha and stir-fry for 1 minute.
5. Add the rice wine mixture and stir until a glaze forms.
6. Add the scallions and stir-fry for 30 seconds.
7. Garnish with the cilantro and serve over jasmine rice.

CHANGE IT UP: *If Smithfield ham is not an option, use ham that has been dry salt cured for at least six months to approximate the long stewing process.*

SICHUAN PORK AND PEPPER WITH PEANUTS

SERVES: 4   **PREP TIME:** 15 minutes   **COOK TIME:** 5 minutes

If you want some real heat, stir-fry this pork dish with hot, dried peppers and mouth-numbing Sichuan peppercorns. The peanuts add a slightly sweet crunchiness that may take the edge off—or at least give you something to chew on while your mouth is cooling down.

- 2 tablespoons cooking oil
- 1 tablespoon crushed, chopped ginger
- 2 garlic cloves, crushed and chopped
- 1 pound ground pork

- 1 medium onion, cut into 1-inch pieces
- 1 teaspoon red pepper flakes
- 1 teaspoon hot sesame oil
- 1 tablespoon Chinese five-spice powder

- 1 medium red bell pepper, cut into 1-inch pieces
- 2 tablespoons rice wine
- 2 tablespoons rice vinegar
- 1 tablespoon cornstarch
- ½ cup peanuts

1. In a wok over high heat, heat the cooking oil until it shimmers.

2. Add the ginger, garlic, pork, and onion and stir-fry for 1 minute.

3. Add the red pepper flakes, sesame oil, five-spice powder, and bell pepper and stir-fry for 1 minute.

4. Add the rice wine, rice vinegar, and cornstarch and stir until a glaze forms.

5. Add the peanuts, stir, and serve over steamed rice.

THAI BASIL PORK

SERVES: 4   **PREP TIME:** 15 minutes   **COOK TIME:** 5 minutes

Fresh basil really adds to the complex umami flavor of the fish and soy sauces. Thai basil is different from sweet basil, which is what is normally grown in the West. The Thai herb is widely used throughout Southeast Asia; it is often described as having an anise- or licorice-like flavor. Thai basil has small, narrow leaves, purple stems, and pink-purple flowers, and it stands up well to stir-frying.

- 2 tablespoons cooking oil
- 1 tablespoon crushed, chopped ginger
- 2 garlic cloves, crushed and chopped
- 1 pound ground pork
- 1 medium red bell pepper, cut into ½-inch pieces
- 1 tablespoon fish sauce
- 2 tablespoons brown sugar
- 1 tablespoon soy sauce
- 1 handful fresh Thai basil leaves

1. In a wok over high heat, heat the cooking oil until it shimmers.
2. Add the ginger, garlic, and pork and stir-fry for 1 minute.
3. Add the bell pepper, fish sauce, brown sugar, and soy sauce and stir-fry for 1 minute.
4. Add the basil and stir-fry until just wilted.
5. Serve over steamed rice.

CHANGE IT UP: *A wedge of lime for each serving provides a nice contrast to the sweet and salty flavor of the sauces and the brown sugar.*

PORK AND EGG DROP SOUP

SERVES: 4　　　　**PREP TIME:** 15 minutes　　　　**COOK TIME:** 8 minutes

Egg Drop Soup reminds me of late-night snacks with my father after my mother and sister went to bed. So, in that sense, it is a comfort food for me. When my children were young and living at home, this recipe is something I made for them, and I still do when they come to visit. Often, Egg Drop Soup is what my wife and I make for each other for Sunday breakfast.

- 3 quarts plus 1¼ cups vegetable or meat broth, divided
- ¼ cup cornstarch
- 1 pound ground pork
- 1 tablespoon crushed, chopped ginger
- 2 garlic cloves, crushed and chopped
- 1 ounce dried, sliced shiitake or tree ear mushrooms
- 4 eggs, beaten
- 1 cup chopped bok choy
- 4 scallions, cut into ½-inch pieces

1. Combine 1 cup of the broth with the cornstarch and stir to form a slurry. Set aside.

2. In a wok over high heat, boil ¼ cup of the broth.

3. Add the pork, ginger, and garlic and cook for 1 minute.

4. Add the remaining 3 quarts broth and the mushrooms to the wok. Bring to a boil.

5. Stir the cornstarch slurry into the boiling broth until the broth thickens.

6. Stir the broth in one direction while drizzling the beaten eggs into the wok.

7. Stir the bok choy into the broth and let cook for 30 seconds.

8. Garnish with the scallions, squeezing them to bruise while dropping them into the broth. Serve immediately.

INGREDIENT TIP: *You can get dried mushrooms at some grocery stores, Asian markets, and online. Look for the sliced versions if possible. If you use whole mushrooms, you'll need to remove them from the broth after rehydrating them to slice before returning them to the broth.*

Coconut Curry Lamb [page 123]

[SEVEN]

BEEF & LAMB

BEEF & LAMB

Beef stir-fry is my favorite dish for entertaining large groups of friends, especially during the summer. We splurge on boneless ribeye steak and thinly slice it up for marinating. Fresh sliced carrots, onions, broccoli, pea pods, and bright peppers are placed in separate large bowls. Freshly prepared ginger and garlic are crushed and chopped. While friends and family are enjoying appetizers and beverages, I heat up my largest cast-iron wok on the outdoor grill until it is glowing hot. Then the show begins. Avocado oil is splashed into the wok, followed quickly by the ginger, garlic, vegetables, and steak. In minutes, the juicy medium-rare steak stir-fry with crispy vegetables is ready to transfer to a serving dish. While guests are lining up to dish out mounds of fluffy steaming rice to go with their fresh stir-fry, I keep the wok hot, splash in some more oil, and start act two. Everyone is as entertained as they are satisfied.

You can make good stir-fry from many cuts of beef, but the better the cut of meat, the better the stir-fry will be. Many recipes suggest flank steak cut across the grain. My preference is to use thinly sliced ribeye steak or well-marbled sirloin tips.

Lamb is a sheep that is less than a year old. Meat from older sheep is called mutton. Good lamb cuts for stir-fry are the rump (also called the chump) and lamb tenderloin. As always, cut across the grain to keep the meat tender. If you want a stronger flavor, try the same cuts of mutton.

BEEF AND BROCCOLI WITH OYSTER SAUCE

SERVES: 4   **PREP TIME:** 15 minutes   **COOK TIME:** 5 minutes

This stir-fry is a favorite Chinese-American takeout dish. Shaoxing rice wine, used in this recipe, is darker and more complex in taste than clear rice wine. Cooking the steak with Shaoxing rice wine also helps tenderize the beef. The combination of umami from the oyster sauce and salty soy sauce makes a great light glaze, keeping the steak tender and moist.

- 2 tablespoons cooking oil
- 1 tablespoon crushed, chopped ginger
- 2 garlic cloves, crushed and chopped
- 1 pound sirloin tips, cut into ¼-inch strips
- 2 tablespoons Shaoxing rice wine
- 1 cup broccoli florets
- 2 tablespoons soy sauce
- ¼ cup oyster sauce

1. In a wok over high heat, heat the cooking oil until it shimmers.
2. Add the ginger and garlic and stir-fry for 30 seconds until lightly browned.
3. Add the steak and rice wine and stir-fry for 1 minute.
4. Add the broccoli and stir-fry for 1 minute.
5. Add the soy sauce and oyster sauce and stir-fry for 1 minute.
6. Serve over steamed rice.

INGREDIENT TIP: *If you can find thinly sliced steak in the meat department, it will make preparation even easier. Remember to let the meat come to room temperature before stir-frying, as cold meat will cool the oil in the wok, resulting in longer searing and cooking time, which will dry out the meat.*

TERIYAKI BEEF AND PEA PODS

SERVES: 4 **PREP TIME:** 15 minutes **COOK TIME:** 6 minutes

Teriyaki is a Japanese cooking technique where the ingredients are stir-fried in a glaze of tamari, mirin, and sugar. The word teriyaki comes from the word teri, which means glaze, and yaki, which means grilling or broiling at high heat. The heat caramelizes both the natural and added sugars to form the glaze.

- 2 tablespoons cooking oil
- 1 tablespoon crushed, chopped ginger
- 2 garlic cloves, crushed and chopped
- 1 pound sirloin tips, cut into ¼-inch strips
- 2 tablespoons tamari
- 2 cups sugar snap or snow pea pods
- 2 tablespoons mirin
- 2 tablespoons brown sugar
- 1 tablespoon cornstarch

1. In a wok over high heat, heat the cooking oil until it shimmers.
2. Add the ginger and garlic and stir-fry for 30 seconds.
3. Add the steak and tamari and stir-fry for 1 minute.
4. Add the pea pods and stir-fry for 1 minute.
5. Add the mirin, sugar, and cornstarch and stir until a light glaze forms.
6. Serve over steamed sushi rice.

INGREDIENT TIP: *Although it's tempting to marinate your steak in the sweet mirin wine, doing this will make it less tender. If you want to marinate with wine, use Shaoxing rice wine and a tablespoon of sugar.*

CRISPY SESAME BEEF

SERVES: 4   **PREP TIME:** 15 minutes   **COOK TIME:** 8 minutes

This stir-fry has an interesting combination of sweet, nutty, and spicy flavors, thanks to the hot sesame oil and chile. A simple breading of cornstarch makes a light, crispy coating for the tasty glaze. You can reduce the spiciness of this dish by replacing the hot sesame oil with regular toasted sesame oil and using a sweet bell pepper in place of the chile.

- ¼ cup soy sauce
- 2 tablespoons rice vinegar
- 2 tablespoons brown sugar
- ¼ cup plus 2 tablespoons cornstarch, divided
- 1 teaspoon hot sesame oil

- 1 pound sirloin steak, thinly sliced
- 1 tablespoon Shaoxing rice wine
- ¼ cup cooking oil
- 1 tablespoon crushed, chopped ginger
- 2 garlic cloves, crushed and chopped

- 1 medium onion, diced
- 1 chile, cut into ¼-inch circles
- 2 tablespoons sesame seeds
- 4 scallions, cut into ½-inch pieces

1. In a small bowl, whisk together the soy sauce, rice vinegar, brown sugar, 2 tablespoons of the cornstarch, and the sesame oil. Set aside.

2. In a large bowl, toss the steak with the rice wine and the remaining ¼ cup of cornstarch, ensuring the steak is coated evenly.

3. In a wok over high heat, heat the cooking oil until it shimmers.

4. Add the ginger and garlic and let it lightly brown for 10 seconds.

5. Shallow-fry (see page 73) the steak until lightly browned, about 1 minute. Remove from the wok and set aside.

6. Remove and discard all but 2 tablespoons of the oil.

7. Add the onion to the wok and stir-fry for 1 minute.

8. Add the chile and stir-fry for 1 minute.

9. Add the soy sauce mixture and stir until a glaze is formed.

10. Return the beef to the wok and stir to coat.

11. Garnish with the sesame seeds and scallions. Serve over rice.

INGREDIENT TIP: *If you don't burn your oil, you can recycle it for later use. Let it cool to room temperature and, using a coffee filter and a funnel, simply return the oil to the original container. Store the oil in an opaque container such as metal or dark glass to protect it from light. If you only have a clear container, place it in a cool cupboard. You can store oil in the refrigerator, for up to three months. Remember to take it out about a half-hour before you're ready to use it so it can come to room temperature.*

JAPANESE BEEF AND RICE (GYUDON)

SERVES: 4 **PREP TIME:** 15 minutes **COOK TIME:** 5 minutes

This minimalist dish was developed in the early 1900s in one of Japan's largest restaurant chains, Yoshinoya. Its simplicity and inexpensive ingredients made it a traditional staple for factory workers. Today, it's perfect for anyone with a busy schedule who still wants a tasty meal.

- 2 tablespoons cooking oil
- 1 tablespoon crushed, chopped ginger
- 2 garlic cloves, crushed and chopped
- 1 medium onion, halved and cut into ¼-inch strips
- ½ cup dashi broth
- 1 tablespoon mirin
- 1 tablespoon sake
- 1 tablespoon tamari
- 1 tablespoon sugar
- 1 pound shaved steak
- 3 scallions, cut into ½-inch pieces

1. In a wok over high heat, heat the cooking oil until it shimmers.
2. Add the ginger, garlic, and onion and stir-fry for 1 minute.
3. Add the dashi, mirin, sake, tamari, and sugar and bring to a boil.
4. Stir in the steak. Add the scallions and stir for 1 minute.
5. Serve over steamed sushi rice.

INGREDIENT TIP: *Dashi broth, a cornerstone of Japanese cooking, is made of water, kombu (dried kelp), and bonito fish flakes. You can buy it as a powder in Asian markets and use it as a base for miso soup, ramen, and more.*

KOREAN GROUND BEEF BOWL WITH KIMCHI

SERVES: 4 **PREP TIME:** 15 minutes **COOK TIME:** 6 minutes

This fast stir-fry dish combines two signature Korean flavors—kimchi and gochujang—for a speedy weeknight meal or late-night snack. Sometimes all it takes is two or three ingredients to add color, texture, and signature flavor to a meal, especially when one ingredient is the national food and the other is the national sauce!

- 2 tablespoons cooking oil
- 1 tablespoon crushed, chopped ginger
- 2 garlic cloves, crushed and chopped
- 1 pound ground beef
- 2 tablespoons soy sauce
- 1 medium onion, diced
- 2 tablespoons gochujang
- 1 cup kimchi
- 1 teaspoon hot sesame oil
- 1 tablespoon sesame seeds
- 4 scallions, cut into ½-inch pieces

1. In a wok over high heat, heat the cooking oil until it shimmers.

2. Add the ginger, garlic, beef, soy sauce, and onion and stir-fry for 1 minute.

3. Stir in the gochujang, kimchi, and sesame oil and stir-fry for 1 minute.

4. Garnish with the sesame seeds and scallions. Serve over steamed rice.

CHANGE IT UP: *You can add broccoli, bok choy, pea pods, or other vegetables to satisfy your palate. Just be sure to add the vegetables that need to be cooked longest before those that need less time in the wok.*

SICHUAN BEEF AND VEGETABLES

SERVES: 4	PREP TIME: 15 minutes	COOK TIME: 6 minutes

Contrary to their name, Sichuan peppercorns are not a kind of pepper. They are the seed pods of the prickly ash tree. The pods are not spicy but have a slight citrus flavor, and their unique numbing effect sets up the heat of the hot chiles.

- 2 tablespoons rice wine
- 2 tablespoons rice vinegar
- 2 tablespoons soy sauce
- 1 tablespoon cornstarch
- 2 tablespoons cooking oil
- 1 tablespoon crushed, chopped ginger
- 2 garlic cloves, crushed and chopped
- 1 pound sirloin steak, cut into ¼-inch strips
- 1 tablespoon Chinese five-spice powder
- 1 medium onion, diced
- 1 teaspoon red pepper flakes
- 2 cups sugar snap or snow pea pods
- 1 teaspoon hot sesame oil
- 4 scallions, cut into 1-inch pieces

1. In a small bowl, whisk together the rice wine, rice vinegar, soy sauce, and cornstarch. Set aside.

2. In a wok over high heat, heat the cooking oil until it shimmers.

3. Add the ginger, garlic, and steak and stir-fry for 1 minute.

4. Add the five-spice powder, onion, and red pepper flakes and stir-fry for 1 minute.

5. Add the pea pods and sesame oil and stir-fry for 1 minute.

6. Add the rice wine mixture and stir-fry until a glaze forms.

7. Garnish with the scallions and serve over rice.

SHA CHA BEEF

SERVES: 4 **PREP TIME:** 15 minutes **COOK TIME:** 6 minutes

Sha cha is a traditional sauce developed in China's northwest province of Gansu. It is a mild, spicy-sweet fermented paste that includes garlic, shrimp, fish, chiles, and soy sauce. Sha cha is referenced in recipes that are over 1,000 years old.

- 2 tablespoons cooking oil
- 1 tablespoon crushed, chopped ginger
- 2 cloves garlic, crushed and chopped
- 1 pound sirloin steak, sliced into ¼-inch strips
- 1 medium onion, cut into 1-inch pieces
- 2 tablespoons soy sauce
- 2 tablespoons Chinese rice wine
- ¼ cup sha cha (see Ingredient Tip)
- 1 chile, cut into ¼-inch circles
- 2 cups sugar snap or snow pea pods
- 4 scallions, cut into 1-inch pieces

1. In a wok over high heat, heat the cooking oil until it shimmers.
2. Add the ginger, garlic, steak, and onion and stir-fry for 1 minute.
3. Add the soy sauce, rice wine, sha cha, and chile and stir-fry for 1 minute.
4. Add the pea pods and stir-fry for 1 minute.
5. Add the scallions and stir-fry for 1 minute.
6. Serve over steamed rice.

INGREDIENT TIP: *Sha cha is often labeled as "Chinese barbecue sauce" in the grocery store. You can also use it as a dipping sauce.*

BEEF RENDANG

SERVES: 4   PREP TIME: 15 minutes   COOK TIME: 8 minutes

This spicy stir-fry is an adaptation of an Indonesian curried beef stew. Using nicely marbled, thinly sliced sirloin steak, rather than lean chunks of stew meat, lets you enjoy the pungent curry flavor in a fraction of the time it takes to cook a pot of beef stew.

- 2 tablespoons coconut oil
- 1 tablespoon crushed, chopped ginger
- 2 garlic cloves, crushed and chopped
- 1 pound sirloin steak, sliced into ¼-inch strips
- 1 teaspoon Chinese five-spice powder

- 1 teaspoon cardamom
- 1 chile, cut into ¼-inch rounds
- Juice of 1 lime
- 1 lemongrass heart (the bottom 2 inches of the white inner layers), minced

- 1 tablespoon brown sugar
- 2 tablespoons soy sauce
- 4 scallions, cut into ½-inch pieces

1. In a wok over high heat, heat the coconut oil until it shimmers.
2. Add the ginger, garlic, steak, five-spice powder, and cardamom and stir-fry for 1 minute.
3. Add the chile, lime juice, lemongrass, brown sugar, and soy sauce and stir-fry for 1 minute.
4. Garnish with the scallions and serve over steamed rice cooked in coconut water or coconut milk.

INGREDIENT TIP: *If you want a stronger lime flavor, you can add the lime zest along with the juice in step 3. Just remember not to use the light part of the rind, as it is bitter.*

MYANMARESE LAMB CURRY

SERVES: 4 **PREP TIME:** 15 minutes **COOK TIME:** 5 minutes

This Myanmarese curry will wake up your taste buds with a combination of spicy, sweet, and sour flavors. Unlike other curries, Myanmarese curry is a simple combination of ginger, garlic, onions, and paprika.

- 2 tablespoons cooking oil
- 2 tablespoons crushed, chopped ginger
- 4 garlic cloves, crushed and chopped
- 1 medium onion, cut into ¼-inch pieces
- 1 tablespoon paprika
- 1 pound boneless leg of lamb or rump, sliced into ¼-inch strips against the grain
- 1 chile, cut into ¼-inch rounds
- 1 tablespoon soy sauce
- 1 tablespoon rice vinegar
- 1 tablespoon brown sugar
- 1 teaspoon hot sesame oil
- 4 scallions, cut into 1-inch pieces

1. In a wok over high heat, heat the cooking oil until it shimmers.
2. Add the ginger, garlic, onion, paprika, and lamb and stir-fry for 1 minute.
3. Add the chile, soy sauce, rice vinegar, and brown sugar and stir-fry for 1 minute.
4. Add the sesame oil and scallions and toss lightly.
5. Serve over steamed rice.

INGREDIENT TIP: *The aromatic rices, jasmine and basmati, are the preferred varieties in Myanmar (formerly known as Burma). The native rice, Pearl Paw San, won a prize for being the best rice in the world and can be found in some Asian markets and online.*

CRYING TIGER LAMB

SERVES: 4 | **PREP TIME:** 15 minutes | **COOK TIME:** 5 minutes

There are two stories about how this spicy Thai dish got its name. The more obvious one is that this dish is so spicy that it will make even the toughest tiger cry when eating it. Another story is that there were two tigers hunting and one tiger gobbled up some tasty meat, causing the other tiger to cry. Either way, this is one spicy stir-fry!

- Juice of 1 lime
- 1 tablespoon brown sugar
- 1 tablespoon hot sesame oil
- 1 tablespoon cornstarch
- 1 pound lamb tenderloin, cut into 1-inch pieces, across the grain
- 1 tablespoon fish sauce
- 1 tablespoon soy sauce
- 2 tablespoons cooking oil
- 1 tablespoon crushed, chopped ginger
- 2 garlic cloves, crushed and chopped
- 1 medium onion, diced
- 2 or 3 Thai bird's eye chiles
- 4 scallions, cut into 1-inch pieces

1. In a small bowl, whisk together the lime juice, brown sugar, sesame oil, and cornstarch. Set aside.

2. In a large bowl, combine the soy sauce and fish sauce. Add the lamb and massage for 1 minute.

3. In a wok over high heat, heat the cooking oil until it shimmers.

4. Add the ginger, garlic, and lamb and stir-fry for 1 minute.

5. Add the onion and bird's eye chiles and stir-fry for 1 minute.

6. Add the lime juice mixture and stir until a glaze forms.

7. Garnish with the scallions and serve over rice.

CHANGE IT UP: *If the bird's eye peppers are too hot for you, substitute jalapeño peppers. If you want it hotter, substitute habanero peppers.*

COCONUT CURRY LAMB

SERVES: 4 **PREP TIME:** 15 minutes **COOK TIME:** 5 minutes

This Thai curried lamb makes use of the hot bird's eye chile and curry paste for pungent heat. The umami of the fish sauce and mushrooms combines nicely with the sweetness of coconut milk and sugar to smooth out the spiciness of this dish.

- 1 tablespoon red Thai curry paste
- ¼ cup canned coconut milk
- 1 tablespoon fish sauce
- 1 tablespoon brown sugar
- 1 tablespoon cornstarch
- 2 tablespoons coconut oil
- 1 tablespoon crushed, chopped ginger
- 2 garlic cloves, crushed and chopped
- 1 pound boneless lamb leg or shoulder, cut into 1-inch pieces
- 1 medium onion, cut into 1-inch pieces
- 4 ounces mushrooms, sliced
- 1 bird's eye chile, thinly sliced
- 2 cups chopped bok choy

1. In a small bowl, whisk together the curry paste, coconut milk, fish sauce, brown sugar, and cornstarch. Set aside.
2. In a wok over high heat, heat the coconut oil until it shimmers.
3. Add the ginger, garlic, and lamb and stir-fry for 1 minute.
4. Add the onion, mushrooms, and bird's eye chile and stir-fry for 1 minute.
5. Add the bok choy and stir-fry for 30 seconds.
6. Add the curry paste mixture and stir until a glaze forms.
7. Serve over coconut rice.

CUMIN LAMB AND PEPPERS

SERVES: 4   **PREP TIME:** 15 minutes   **COOK TIME:** 5 minutes

This recipe has its roots deep within the northwestern Chinese province of Xinjiang, where lamb and mutton are the favorite meats. However, the combination of lamb and cumin has become very popular all over China. Perhaps that popularity will expand to your table, too!

- 2 tablespoons cooking oil
- 1 tablespoon crushed, chopped ginger
- 2 garlic cloves, crushed and chopped
- 1 pound boneless leg of lamb or shoulder, cut into 1-inch pieces
- 1 medium onion, diced
- 1 tablespoon ground cumin or cumin seeds
- ½ teaspoon ground black pepper
- ¼ teaspoon kosher salt
- 1 red bell pepper, cut into ½-inch pieces
- 1 tablespoon rice wine
- 1 tablespoon rice vinegar
- 2 tablespoons soy sauce
- 1 tablespoon cornstarch
- ½ cup coarsely chopped cilantro

1. In a wok over high heat, heat the cooking oil until it shimmers.
2. Add the ginger, garlic, and lamb and stir-fry for 1 minute.
3. Add the onion, cumin, black pepper, and salt and stir-fry for 1 minute.
4. Add the bell pepper and stir-fry for 1 minute.
5. Add the rice wine, rice vinegar, soy sauce, and cornstarch and stir until a glaze forms.
6. Garnish with the cilantro and serve over steamed rice.

ADOBO LAMB AND CABBAGE

SERVES: 4   **PREP TIME:** 15 minutes   **COOK TIME:** 8 minutes

In the Philippines, "adobo" refers to a cooking method rather than a specific seasoning. Adobo is a favorite Filipino way of stewing meat in a sweet-sour-hot broth. In this easy stir-fry adaptation, we'll repurpose that tangy broth as a light glaze to coat stir-fried lamb, giving it a hot and sour flavor while keeping it moist and tender.

- 2 tablespoons soy sauce
- ¼ cup rice vinegar
- 2 tablespoons brown sugar
- 2 tablespoons cornstarch
- 1 cup Napa cabbage, shredded
- 2 tablespoons cooking oil
- 1 tablespoon crushed, chopped ginger
- 2 garlic cloves, crushed and chopped
- 1 pound boneless leg of lamb or shoulder, cut into ¼-inch strips
- 1 medium onion, diced
- 1 teaspoon red pepper flakes

1. In a small bowl, whisk together the soy sauce, rice vinegar, brown sugar, and cornstarch. Set aside.
2. In a wok over high heat, heat the cooking oil until it shimmers.
3. Add the ginger, garlic, lamb, onion, and red pepper flakes and stir-fry for 1 minute.
4. Add the soy sauce mixture and cabbage and stir until a glaze forms.
5. Serve over steamed rice.

INGREDIENT TIP: *For a recipe shortcut, Filipino adobo sauce can be found at some Asian markets and online. Just be sure it's Filipino adobo sauce and not Mexican adobo powder.*

GROUND LAMB AND GREEN BEANS

SERVES: 4   **PREP TIME:** 15 minutes   **COOK TIME:** 5 minutes

This is a very fast and healthy stir-fry. Lamb is considered by many to be the healthiest red meat, as it has higher levels of "good" fats than other red meats. Using ground lamb allows it to absorb the flavors of the ginger and garlic, while the glaze blends the five spices, hot sesame oil, and oyster sauce for a great-tasting dish.

- 2 tablespoons cooking oil
- 1 tablespoon crushed, chopped ginger
- 2 garlic cloves, crushed and chopped
- 1 pound ground lamb
- 1 medium onion, diced
- 2 cups fresh green beans
- 1 tablespoon Chinese five-spice powder
- 1 teaspoon hot sesame oil
- ¼ cup oyster sauce

1. In a wok over high heat, heat the cooking oil until it shimmers.
2. Add the ginger, garlic, lamb, and onion and stir-fry for 1 minute.
3. Add the green beans, five-spice powder, and sesame oil and stir-fry for 1 minute.
4. Add the oyster sauce and stir-fry for 1 minute.
5. Serve over steamed rice.

CHANGE IT UP: *You can substitute any ground meat or even crumbled extra-firm tofu for the lamb, if desired. For a fully vegetarian meal, use vegetarian oyster sauce, mushroom sauce, or hoisin sauce. Frozen green beans can be substituted for fresh in a pinch.*

HOT AND SOUR BEEF AND BOK CHOY SOUP

SERVES: 4   **PREP TIME:** 15 minutes   **COOK TIME:** 8 minutes

This is a great everyday soup that can be put together quickly. Stir-frying the carrots and onions caramelizes their natural sugars, making them very sweet and tender. Also note that there's no need to wait for the broth to cook them through. Moreover, the shaved meat cooks in 5 to 10 seconds if the broth is actively boiling.

- 2 tablespoons cooking oil
- 1 tablespoon crushed chopped ginger
- 2 garlic cloves, crushed and chopped
- 1 medium carrot, julienned
- 1 medium onion, cut into 1-inch pieces
- 4 ounces mushrooms, sliced
- 3 quarts vegetable or meat broth
- 1 teaspoon hot sesame oil
- ¼ cup rice vinegar
- 1 cup chopped bok choy
- 1 pound shaved steak

1. In a wok over high heat, heat the cooking oil until it shimmers.
2. Add the ginger, garlic, and carrot and stir-fry for 30 seconds.
3. Add the onion and mushrooms and stir-fry for 30 seconds.
4. Add the broth, sesame oil, and rice vinegar and bring to a boil.
5. Add the bok choy and steak and stir for 30 seconds.
6. Serve immediately.

CHANGE IT UP: *If you have the time, you can heat up the broth in a saucepan and rehydrate dried shiitake or tree ear mushrooms for 15 minutes. I suggest using sliced dried shiitakes, as they cost the same by weight as whole mushrooms and will hydrate faster. The texture and flavor of dried mushrooms is more robust than fresh mushrooms.*

Pancit Canton [page 146]

[EIGHT]

NOODLE & FRIED RICE DISHES

NOODLE & FRIED RICE DISHES

Rice and noodles are the most popular staple foods in Asia. Rice is a type of grass that was domesticated over 13,000 years ago along the Yangtze River in China. Its cultivation spread across Asia to the Middle East, Africa, Europe, and the Americas. Rice provides vitamins, minerals, and carbohydrates, and brown and colored rices provide additional nutrients due to less processing and the retention of fiber. Fried rice is best made from cold leftover rice. This prevents the rice from overcooking and becoming mushy while being stir-fried with other ingredients.

Archaeologists excavated an upside-down bowl of 4,000-year-old noodles made from millet in Lajia, northwestern China. Today, noodles are mostly made from wheat or rice flour and come in a variety of widths. The flour may be combined with water or eggs to create the noodles, which are quickly boiled and incorporated into many stir-fry recipes.

Most Asian noodles are sold dried. Fresh noodles can be found in the refrigerated cases of some grocery stores and in Asian markets. Since there are so many varieties, it is best to follow the package instructions when preparing them. When cooking noodles, you want to undercook them until they are just al dente, firm but flexible. Always bring the water to boiling before putting the noodles in to cook; otherwise, they will become soggy and mushy. The thicker the noodle, the longer it will take to cook. Keep in mind that dry noodles will take twice as long as fresh soft noodles to cook.

SHRIMP FRIED RICE

SERVES: 4   **PREP TIME:** 15 minutes   **COOK TIME:** 5 minutes

Fried rice is the perfect recipe when you're trying to make the most of what's sitting in your fridge from earlier meals. I'm always amazed at how far the contents of three or four small takeout containers can go, and how delicious they can be together. But that's not to say that you have to wait for leftovers to whip up a wok full of this tasty goodness; try this stir-fry whenever you get a comfort food craving! Feel free to use any type of sesame oil you have on hand.

- 2 tablespoons cooking oil
- 1 tablespoon crushed, chopped ginger
- 2 garlic cloves, crushed and chopped
- ½ teaspoon kosher salt

- 2 large eggs, beaten
- 1 medium onion, diced
- ½ pound medium shrimp, peeled, deveined, and halved lengthwise

- 1 cup frozen peas, thawed
- 2 cups cold, cooked rice
- 1 teaspoon sesame oil
- 1 tablespoon soy sauce
- 4 scallions, cut into ½-inch pieces

1. In a wok over high heat, heat the cooking oil until it shimmers.

2. Add the ginger, garlic, salt, and eggs and stir-fry for 1 minute, or until the eggs are firm.

3. Add the onion and shrimp and stir-fry for 1 minute.

4. Add the peas, rice, sesame oil, and soy sauce and stir-fry for 1 minute.

5. Garnish with the scallions and serve immediately.

INGREDIENT TIP: *Fried rice works best with leftover day-old rice. It dries out a little and is less sticky, and the flavor will be more pronounced when fried.*

VEGETABLE FRIED RICE

SERVES: 4 | **PREP TIME:** 15 minutes | **COOK TIME:** 8 minutes

This recipe is an easy and delicious way to use up what you have in your refrigerator. Grab that day-old rice, your leftover veggies, and that last handful of frozen peas, corn, or carrots. Add a couple of eggs and you're ready to start dinner!

- 2 tablespoons cooking oil
- 1 tablespoon crushed, chopped ginger
- 2 garlic cloves, crushed and chopped
- ½ teaspoon kosher salt
- 4 large eggs, beaten
- 1 medium carrot, julienned
- 1 medium onion, diced
- 1 red bell pepper, diced
- 1 cup frozen peas, thawed
- 2 cups cold, cooked rice
- 1 teaspoon sesame oil
- 1 tablespoon soy sauce
- 4 scallions, cut into ½-inch pieces

1. In a wok over high heat, heat the cooking oil until it shimmers.
2. Add the ginger, garlic, salt, and eggs and stir-fry for 1 minute, or until the eggs are firm.
3. Add the carrot and stir-fry for 1 minute.
4. Add the onion and stir-fry for 1 minute.
5. Add the bell pepper and stir-fry for 1 minute.
6. Add the peas, rice, sesame oil, and soy sauce and stir-fry for 1 minute.
7. Garnish with the scallions and serve immediately.

CHANGE IT UP: *You can make this recipe vegan and gluten-free by replacing the scrambled eggs with crumbled tofu and using gluten-free tamari or soy sauce.*

KIMCHI FRIED RICE

SERVES: 4   **PREP TIME:** 15 minutes   **COOK TIME:** 8 minutes

This is a fun way to use up that last bit of kimchi fermenting in the back of your refrigerator. Kimchi gets more sour and softer with age, so distributing its flavor among the fried rice ingredients is a great way to mellow it out. The thick-sliced bacon is a decadent addition to this tasty dish.

- ½ pound thick-sliced bacon, cut into 1-inch pieces
- 1 tablespoon crushed, chopped ginger
- 2 garlic cloves, crushed and chopped
- 4 ounces sliced mushrooms
- 1 cup kimchi, cut into ½-inch pieces
- 2 cups cold, cooked rice
- 1 teaspoon sesame oil
- 4 scallions, cut into ½-inch pieces
- 1 tablespoon soy sauce
- ¼ cup kimchi juice
- 4 large eggs

1. Place the bacon, ginger, and garlic in a wok over high heat and stir-fry for 2 minutes, or until the bacon is lightly browned.

2. Drain off all but 2 tablespoons of the bacon fat from the wok and set aside.

3. Add the mushrooms to the wok and stir-fry for 1 minute.

4. Add the kimchi and stir-fry for 30 seconds.

5. Add the rice, sesame oil, scallions, soy sauce, and kimchi juice. Stir-fry for 30 seconds, then remove from the wok and place on a serving dish.

6. Return 2 tablespoons of the reserved bacon fat to the wok and fry the eggs sunny-side up.

7. Serve the rice with the fried eggs on top.

PREPARATION TIPS: *Feel free to use regular bacon instead of thick-sliced bacon. Kimchi that is a week old or more will provide more juice but will be softer.*

INDONESIAN FRIED RICE (NASI GORENG)

SERVES: 4 **PREP TIME:** 15 minutes **COOK TIME:** 8 minutes

Nasi goreng means "fried rice" in Malaysian and Indonesian. This is a very simple dish with a little meat, onions, and a sweet soy sauce known as kecap manis. Nasi goreng is usually served with a fried egg on top, sliced tomatoes, and cucumbers on the side.

- 3 tablespoons cooking oil, divided
- ½ pound ground meat of your choice
- 1 tablespoon crushed, chopped ginger
- 2 garlic cloves, crushed and chopped
- 1 medium onion, diced
- 2 cups cold, cooked rice
- ¼ cup kecap manis
- 1 teaspoon hot sesame oil
- 4 scallions, cut into ½-inch pieces
- 4 eggs
- 2 tomatoes, sliced
- 1 cucumber, sliced

1. In a wok over high heat, heat 2 tablespoons of the cooking oil until it shimmers.

2. Add the meat, ginger, garlic, and onion and stir-fry for 1 minute.

3. Add the rice, kecap manis, sesame oil, and scallions and stir-fry for 1 minute. Remove from the wok and place in a serving bowl.

4. Add the remaining 1 tablespoon of cooking oil to the wok and, when the oil is shimmering, fry the eggs sunny-side up.

5. Serve each portion of rice with a fried egg on top, and sliced tomatoes and cucumbers on the side.

INGREDIENT TIP: *You can find kecap manis in the international section of some grocery stores, Asian markets, and online. Or you can make your own by simmering ¼ cup of regular soy sauce and stirring in ¼ cup of brown sugar until it dissolves and thickens. Let the sauce cool before using, as it will thicken as it sits.*

INDIAN FRIED RICE (FODNI BHAAT)

SERVES: 4   **PREP TIME:** 10 minutes   **COOK TIME:** 4 minutes

Fodni bhaat means "tempered rice" or "seasoned rice." As with most fried rice recipes, it is an excellent way to use leftover rice. There's a saying in India that if someone brings fodni bhaat to work, they were late for dinner and are eating last night's leftovers for lunch.

- 2 tablespoons cooking oil
- 1 tablespoon crushed, chopped ginger
- 1 medium onion, diced
- 1 teaspoon mustard seeds
- 2 garlic cloves, crushed and chopped
- 2 bird's eye chiles, sliced into ¼-inch circles
- 1 teaspoon hot sesame oil
- ½ teaspoon turmeric
- ½ teaspoon ground coriander
- ¼ teaspoon kosher salt
- 2 cups cold, cooked basmati rice
- ¼ cup coarsely chopped mint leaves

1. In a wok over high heat, heat the cooking oil until it shimmers.

2. Add the ginger, onion, mustard seeds, and garlic to the wok and stir-fry for 1 minute.

3. Add the bird's eye chiles, sesame oil, turmeric, coriander, salt, and rice and stir-fry for 1 minute.

4. Garnish with the mint and serve immediately.

JAPANESE FRIED RICE (YAKIMESHI)

SERVES: 4   **PREP TIME:** 15 minutes   **COOK TIME:** 8 minutes

Yes, you guessed it—yakimeshi means "fried rice" in Japanese. It is an excellent way to use up leftovers and can be as simple as some leftover sushi rice, a scrambled egg, and some chopped scallions. Or it can involve meat, seafood, several vegetables, and spices. This recipe is right in the middle.

- ½ pound thick-sliced bacon, cut into 1-inch pieces
- 1 tablespoon crushed, chopped ginger
- 2 garlic cloves, crushed and chopped
- 3 eggs, beaten
- 2 cups cold, cooked rice
- 1 teaspoon sesame oil
- 4 scallions, cut into ½-inch pieces
- 2 tablespoons sesame seeds
- Kosher salt
- Ground black pepper

1. In a wok over high heat, stir-fry the bacon, ginger, and garlic for 2 minutes, or until the bacon is lightly browned.
2. Remove the bacon and set aside.
3. Add the eggs and stir-fry until they are firm and dry.
4. Add the cooked bacon, rice, and sesame oil and stir-fry for 1 minute.
5. Add the scallions and sesame seeds and toss for 30 seconds.
6. Serve with salt and pepper to taste.

CHANGE IT UP: *Some yakimeshi recipes call for mixing a tablespoon of mayonnaise into the rice before stir-frying it to help separate the grains and add another flavor. Try it for yourself to see if you like it!*

SINANGAG

SERVES: 4   **PREP TIME:** 15 minutes   **COOK TIME:** 6 minutes

This Filipino recipe for garlic fried rice is a lightning-fast, delectable side dish. Sinangag uses only four ingredients, plus cooking oil, which are almost certainly in your kitchen right now. The preferred rice is an aromatic long-grain variety such as jasmine or basmati that is at least a day old. Due to the dish's strong flavor, other meats and vegetables are not included. It is typically served alongside other dishes, so the diner can control how much garlic flavor to mix into their meal.

- 2 tablespoons cooking oil
- 8 cloves garlic, crushed and chopped
- 2 cups cold, cooked rice
- ¼ teaspoon kosher salt
- 4 scallions, cut into ¼-inch pieces

1. In a wok over medium-high heat, heat the cooking oil and garlic. Stir-fry for 2 minutes until the garlic turns golden brown but does not burn.

2. Remove half the garlic and reserve it for garnishing.

3. Gently sprinkle the rice and salt into the wok and stir-fry for 1 minute.

4. Garnish with the chopped scallions and caramelized garlic before serving.

PREPARATION TIP: *The key to this fried rice is to brown the garlic without burning it, allowing for caramelization of the natural sugars. This reduces the garlic's pungency and increases its sweetness.*

CHINESE SAUSAGE FRIED RICE

SERVES: 4   **PREP TIME:** 15 minutes   **COOK TIME:** 8 minutes

This fried rice recipe makes use of cured Chinese sausage. Lap cheong is a southern Chinese sausage usually made from pork or beef cured with generous amounts of fat, salt, and sugar. Think of lap cheong as a Chinese version of dry-cured bacon.

- 1 tablespoon cooking oil
- 1 tablespoon crushed, chopped ginger
- 2 garlic cloves, crushed and chopped
- 2 links cured Chinese sausage, sliced into ½-inch pieces
- 2 large eggs, beaten
- 1 cup frozen peas, thawed
- 2 cups cold, cooked rice
- 1 tablespoon sesame oil
- 2 tablespoons soy sauce
- 4 scallions, cut into ½-inch pieces

1. In a wok over high heat, heat the cooking oil until it shimmers.
2. Add the ginger, garlic, and sausage and stir-fry for 1 minute.
3. Push the sausage to the sides of the wok, add the eggs, and stir-fry for 1 minute.
4. Add the peas, rice, sesame oil, and soy sauce and stir-fry for 1 minute.
5. Garnish with the scallions and serve immediately.

INGREDIENT TIP: *You can find cured Chinese sausage in the refrigerated section of Asian markets and online. The fatty, uncured Chinese sausage found in grocery stores can be used but will impart a different flavor.*

VEGETABLE CHOW MEIN

SERVES: 4   **PREP TIME:** 15 minutes   **COOK TIME:** 6 minutes

Chow mein means "fried noodles" in Cantonese and originated in northern China. The version we know and love has been modified to fit Western tastes; initially, the dish was made with stir-fried vegetables and boiled noodles. In this recipe, the cooked noodles, or mein, are fried until they are firm and somewhat chewy before being added to the other ingredients.

- ¼ cup cooking oil
- 1 pound cooked noodles
- 1 tablespoon crushed, chopped ginger
- 2 garlic cloves, crushed and chopped
- 1 medium onion, cut into 1-inch pieces
- 1 red bell pepper, cut into 1-inch pieces
- 2 cups sugar snap or snow pea pods
- ¼ cup hoisin sauce
- 2 tablespoons honey
- 2 tablespoons soy sauce
- 2 tablespoons Shaoxing rice wine
- 4 scallions, cut into 1-inch pieces

1. In a wok over high heat, heat the cooking oil until it shimmers.
2. Add the noodles and stir-fry for 2 minutes until lightly browned.
3. Remove the noodles and drain off all but 2 tablespoons of oil.
4. Add the ginger, garlic, and onion to the wok and stir-fry for 1 minute.
5. Add the bell pepper and pea pods and stir-fry for 1 minute.
6. Add the noodles, hoisin sauce, honey, soy sauce, and rice wine and stir-fry for 1 minute.
7. Garnish with the scallions and serve.

INGREDIENT TIP: *There are dozens of choices for noodles out there. By far the most common types are wheat- and egg-based noodles. They are available dried, frozen, and fresh. You can get them in a variety of widths, styles, and flavors, but all are boiled before being used in recipes.*

SEAFOOD LO MEIN

SERVES: 4   **PREP TIME:** 15 minutes   **COOK TIME:** 6 minutes

Lo mein means "stirred noodles" in Cantonese. Unlike chow mein, where the noodles are fried before mixing them in with the other ingredients, the cooked noodles in lo mein are incorporated with the ingredients during the stir-frying process, producing more tender noodles.

- 2 tablespoons cooking oil
- 1 tablespoon crushed, chopped ginger
- 2 garlic cloves, crushed and chopped
- ¼ pound ground pork
- 1 medium onion, cut into 1-inch pieces
- 1 red bell pepper, cut into 1-inch pieces
- ¼ pound medium shrimp, peeled, deveined, and cut in half lengthwise
- ¼ pound sea scallops, cut in half widthwise
- 2 tablespoons soy sauce
- 2 tablespoons rice wine
- ¼ cup oyster sauce
- 1 pound cooked noodles

1. In a wok over high heat, heat the cooking oil until it shimmers.
2. Add the ginger, garlic, pork, and onion and stir-fry for 1 minute.
3. Add the bell pepper and shrimp and stir-fry for 1 minute.
4. Add the scallops and stir-fry for 30 seconds.
5. In a small bowl, whisk together the soy sauce, rice wine, and oyster sauce, then add the mixture to the wok.
6. Add the noodles and stir-fry for 30 seconds.
7. Serve immediately.

PAD THAI CHICKEN

SERVES: 4　　　　**PREP TIME:** 15 minutes　　　　**COOK TIME:** 6 minutes

Pad Thai was invented in the 1930s by the prime minister of Thailand specifically to be a symbol and source of national and cultural pride, and quickly became wildly popular. Its ingredients reflect, in a very simple way, the flavors and ingredients of Thailand. The umami of fish sauce, fresh lime juice, tart tamarind, hot peppers, rice noodles, and cilantro are all native to Thailand.

- 2 tablespoons tamarind paste
- 1 tablespoon fish sauce
- 1 tablespoon soy sauce
- 2 tablespoons brown sugar
- 1 tablespoon cornstarch
- 2 tablespoons cooking oil

- 1 tablespoon crushed, chopped ginger
- 2 garlic cloves, crushed and chopped
- 2 eggs, beaten
- 1 pound boneless chicken thighs, cut into 1-inch pieces

- 2 bird's eye chiles, sliced into ¼-inch circles
- 1 pound cooked rice noodles
- ½ cup chopped peanuts
- 1 cup bean sprouts
- Coarsely chopped cilantro
- Lime wedges

1. In a small bowl, whisk together the tamarind paste, fish sauce, soy sauce, brown sugar, and cornstarch. Set aside.

2. In a wok over high heat, heat the cooking oil until it shimmers.

3. Add the ginger, garlic, and eggs and stir-fry for 1 minute.

4. Add the chicken and bird's eye chiles and stir-fry for 1 minute.

5. Add the tamarind paste mixture and stir until a glaze forms.

6. Serve over the noodles and garnish with the peanuts, bean sprouts, cilantro, and lime wedges.

INGREDIENT TIP: *Tamarind is a tangy, sticky paste gathered from the seed pods of the tamarind tree, which is a large tropical tree native to Africa but grows all over Asia as well. Tamarind paste can be found in Asian markets and online and keeps very well in the refrigerator. If you can't find tamarind, you can substitute 2 tablespoons of lime juice or vinegar along with 2 tablespoons of brown sugar for each teaspoon of tamarind.*

PEANUT SESAME NOODLES

SERVES: 4 **PREP TIME:** 15 minutes **COOK TIME:** 5 minutes

When you taste this super-fast and easy noodle stir-fry, your taste buds will experience three distinct flavors. First, there will be a rich, nutty taste from the peanut butter and sesame oil. Second is the sweetness of the sugar. Finally, the spiciness of the hot sesame oil will finish each mouthful. Yum!

- ¼ cup peanut butter
- ¼ cup peanut oil
- 1 tablespoon hot sesame oil
- 2 tablespoons powdered sugar
- 2 tablespoons soy sauce
- 2 tablespoons cooking oil
- 1 tablespoon crushed, chopped ginger
- 2 garlic cloves, crushed and chopped
- 1 pound cooked noodles
- 4 scallions, cut into ½-inch pieces
- 1 tablespoon sesame seeds

1. In a medium bowl, whisk together the peanut butter, peanut oil, sesame oil, powdered sugar, and soy sauce until smooth. Set aside.
2. In a wok over high heat, heat the cooking oil until it shimmers.
3. Add the ginger, garlic, and noodles and stir-fry for 1 minute.
4. Add the peanut butter mixture and toss for 30 seconds.
5. Garnish with the scallions and sesame seeds and serve.

PORK AND CABBAGE HAKKA NOODLES

SERVES: 4   **PREP TIME:** 15 minutes   **COOK TIME:** 6 minutes

Hakka noodles are very similar to chow mein. Both are Chinese recipes, but hakka noodles have been influenced by Indonesian and Indian flavors. Hakka noodles are not as crispy as chow mein but not as soft as lo mein.

- 2 tablespoons cooking oil
- 1 tablespoon crushed, chopped ginger
- 2 garlic cloves, crushed and chopped
- 1 pound ground pork
- 1 medium carrot, julienned
- 1 medium onion, diced
- 1 cup shredded cabbage
- 1 pound cooked noodles
- 1 tablespoon fish sauce
- 1 tablespoon soy sauce
- 1 tablespoon hoisin sauce
- 1 teaspoon ground coriander
- 1 teaspoon hot sesame oil
- 1 scallion, cut into ½-inch pieces

1. In a wok over high heat, heat the oil until it shimmers.
2. Add the ginger, garlic, and pork and stir-fry for 1 minute.
3. Add the carrot, onion, and cabbage and stir-fry for 1 minute.
4. Add the noodles and stir-fry for 1 minute.
5. Add the fish sauce, soy sauce, hoisin, coriander, and sesame oil and stir-fry for 1 minute.
6. Garnish with the scallion and serve.

PREPARATION TIPS: *Heavily salt your water when boiling noodles for the best flavor. You should use 2 tablespoons of kosher salt per gallon of water. Don't worry, the noodles will not absorb a lot of salt in the short time they are cooking in the water. Also remember, you don't want to overcook the noodles. They should be al dente; when you bite into one of the noodles, there should be some resistance and the very center of the noodle will be lighter-colored than the outside.*

PANCIT CANTON

SERVES: 4   **PREP TIME:** 15 minutes   **COOK TIME:** 8 minutes

Pancit canton means "Cantonese noodles" in Filipino and is the Filipino version of lo mein, or stirred noodles. This recipe calls for thin, precooked wheat noodles called Hong Kong-style noodles. They are added at the end of the cooking process to soften and absorb all the flavors from the ingredients and the sauces.

- 2 tablespoons cooking oil
- 1 tablespoon crushed, chopped ginger
- 2 garlic cloves, crushed and chopped
- ¼ pound boneless chicken thighs, cut into 1-inch pieces
- 1 medium carrot, julienned

- ¼ pound thinly sliced sirloin steak, cut into 1-inch pieces
- 1 medium onion, cut into 1-inch pieces
- 4 ounces shiitake mushrooms, sliced
- ¼ pound medium shrimp, peeled, deveined, and cut in half lengthwise

- 1 tablespoon fish sauce
- 2 tablespoons soy sauce
- ¼ cup oyster sauce
- ¼ cup meat or vegetable broth
- 1 pound cooked Hong Kong-style noodles
- 4 scallions, cut into 1-inch pieces
- Lemon wedges

1. In a wok over high heat, heat the oil until it shimmers.
2. Add the ginger, garlic, chicken, and carrot and stir-fry for 1 minute.
3. Add the steak, onion, and mushrooms and stir-fry for 1 minute.
4. Add the shrimp, fish sauce, soy sauce, oyster sauce, and broth and stir-fry for 1 minute.
5. Add the noodles and stir-fry for 1 minute.
6. Garnish with the scallions and serve with the lemon wedges.

INGREDIENT TIP: *Pre-cooked Hong Kong-style, or pan-fried, noodles can be found in the refrigerated section of some grocery stores and in Asian markets. You can also find them frozen and dried, but in these instances you will need to cook them before stir-frying.*

HOT AND SOUR GLASS NOODLE SOUP

SERVES: 4   **PREP TIME:** 15 minutes   **COOK TIME:** 8 minutes

This hearty hot and sour noodle soup gets its flavor from rice vinegar and hot sesame oil. The thin, slippery glass or cellophane noodles are perfect for soaking up the flavorful broth created by the aromatic ginger and garlic—and for slurping! When eating, be sure to break the soft-poached egg yolks to add even more rich flavor.

- 2 tablespoons cooking oil
- 1 tablespoon crushed, chopped ginger
- 2 garlic cloves, crushed and chopped
- ½ pound ground pork

- 1 medium carrot, julienned
- 3 quarts meat or vegetable broth
- 8 ounces dry vermicelli glass noodles
- ¼ cup rice vinegar

- 1 teaspoon hot sesame oil
- 4 eggs, cracked into a bowl with yolks unbroken
- 1 cup chopped bok choy
- 1 scallion, cut into ½-inch pieces

1. In a wok over high heat, heat the cooking oil until it shimmers.

2. Add the ginger, garlic, pork, and carrot and stir-fry for 1 minute.

3. Add the broth, noodles, rice vinegar, and sesame oil and bring to a boil.

4. Distribute the eggs into the boiling broth without breaking the yolks and poach for 1 minute.

5. Sprinkle the bok choy into the soup and let it cook for 1 minute.

6. Garnish with the scallion and serve with one poached egg in each bowl.

INGREDIENT TIP: *Glass noodles are made from the starch of mung beans, potatoes, sweet potatoes, or tapioca. They are opaque before they cook up in the broth. They can be mistaken for thin rice noodles, so check the ingredients if you're not sure. Although they can be used for soup, the rice noodles won't become clear when cooked. You can find the glass noodles in the international section of most grocery stores, in Asian markets, and online.*

COOK TIME CHEAT SHEET

This chart contains several common ingredients used in this cookbook. The indicated cook times can be used as a guide when mixing and matching ingredients, keeping in mind that those that require longer cooking time should be placed in the wok earlier than those that will cook more quickly. I encourage you to use this chart to experiment and create your own versions of these and other new recipes!

INGREDIENT	COOK TIME (HIGH HEAT)	TIPS
Chicken	6 minutes	If coated in cornstarch, cook 1 minute longer in more oil for shallow frying. Cut across the grain.
Pork	5 minutes	Cut across the grain. Tenderloin and butt are good cuts for stir-frying.
Beef	3 minutes	Cut across the grain. Thin-sliced sirloin and sirloin tips are great for stir-frying. Flank steak and chuck are good if on a budget.
Lamb	3 minutes	Be careful not to overcook lamb, as it dries out easily. Rump and tenderloin are good for stir-frying.

INGREDIENT	COOK TIME (HIGH HEAT)	TIPS
Fish	3 minutes	Use firmer fish for stir-frying, such as cod, haddock, salmon, tuna, swordfish, and hake.
Shrimp	3 minutes	After shelling and deveining shrimp, cut them in half lengthwise. They will curl into spirals when cooked.
Scallops	2 minutes	Whenever possible, use fresh "dry" scallops that are not treated with preservative chemicals.
Squid	2 minutes	Squid should be cooked for a maximum of 2 minutes, just until the tentacles curl.
Tofu	6 minutes	Use firm, dry tofu for stir-frying. If you freeze and drain extra-firm tofu, it will become firmer. Use silken tofu to replace scrambled eggs.
Rice	15-40 minutes	When timing rice for cooking, start when the water is boiling. Keep the steam in the pot. Do not remove the cover to check the rice until the cook time is up. See page 20 for more rice-cooking tips.

INGREDIENT	COOK TIME (HIGH HEAT)	TIPS
Noodles	2-10 minutes	When boiling dried noodles, bring the water to a boil before placing the noodles in the water. It's better to slightly undercook noodles so they are al dente. The heat of the wok and any liquid from the stir-fry will further soften them.
Ginger	1-2 minutes	When possible, use fresh ginger. Look for tubers with slightly shiny skin. There's no need to peel ginger for stir-frying. Cut ¼-inch circles across the grain to smash and chop.
Garlic	1-2 minutes	When possible, use fresh garlic. Smashing and chopping peeled cloves quickly releases the flavor and aroma. Be careful not to burn garlic. Stir-fry with other ingredients like ginger, carrots, onions, and meat.
Scallions	1-2 minutes	If using scallions as a garnish, you can bruise them by squeezing them before sprinkling them. The white part has a stronger flavor than the green. Slicing them finely or at an angle releases more flavor.

INGREDIENT	COOK TIME (HIGH HEAT)	TIPS
Lemongrass		The inner stalk of lemongrass is used to impart a citrus flavor to recipes. It can be cut into 1-inch pieces and bruised before cooking to release its aroma, then removed before serving. Lemongrass can also be minced and mixed in with the other ingredients.
Tamari		Think of tamari as the Japanese version of soy sauce. It is a byproduct of making miso. It is less salty and has more umami flavor than soy sauce.
Cooking Wine		The best-known brand of Chinese cooking wine, or rice wine, is Shaoxing. It is used for tenderizing and flavoring meats for stir-frying. Japanese cooking wine, or mirin, is a very sweet, syrupy wine used for flavoring. It is generally not used to marinate for more than a minute, as it firms up the texture of meats.
Soy Sauce		There are two basic types of soy sauce: light and dark/sweet. Light or regular soy sauce is saltier. Dark/sweet soy sauce contains sugar and other thickeners.
Fish Sauce		Thai fish sauce is stronger and saltier than Vietnamese fish sauce. Refrigeration is not required.

FLAVOR BASE BY COUNTRY

To help you make your own stir-fry dishes inspired by the diverse flavors of various Asian cuisines, I have included a chart detailing the flavor bases most common in different countries' culinary traditions. Please note that this is not all-inclusive, as there is substantial variety in cuisines even within countries; this chart is simply meant to serve as an aid in your cooking journey. I encourage you to continue to learn as much as you can about these rich culinary traditions, as well as continue experimenting with your own creations!

COUNTRY	FLAVOR BASE	OTHER COMMON INGREDIENTS
China	Garlic, ginger, scallions, soy sauce	Shaoxing wine, black bean sauce, sesame oil
India	Ginger, onions, garlic, chiles	Ghee, curry, cumin, cardamom
Japan	Tamari, ginger, dashi, miso	Mirin, rice vinegar, sake, garlic
Korea	Gochujang, garlic, chiles, kimchi	Soy sauce, sesame oil
Malaysia	Cumin, fennel, sambal oelek	Coconut, oyster sauce, chiles
Myanmar	Chiles, ginger, fish paste	Curry, mango, pork, basil, garlic, lime
Philippines	Garlic, onion, chiles, ginger	Oyster sauce, lemongrass
Thailand	Shallots, garlic, chiles, lime	Lemongrass, coconut, basil, fish sauce
Vietnam	Fish sauce, ginger, garlic	Lime, lemongrass, cilantro

MEASUREMENT CONVERSIONS

VOLUME EQUIVALENTS	U.S. STANDARD	U.S. STANDARD (OUNCES)	METRIC (APPROXIMATE)
Liquid	2 tablespoons	1 fl. oz.	30 mL
	¼ cup	2 fl. oz.	60 mL
	½ cup	4 fl. oz.	120 mL
	1 cup	8 fl. oz.	240 mL
	1½ cups	12 fl. oz.	355 mL
	2 cups or 1 pint	16 fl. oz.	475 mL
	4 cups or 1 quart	32 fl. oz.	1 L
	1 gallon	128 fl. oz.	4 L
Dry	⅛ teaspoon	–	0.5 mL
	¼ teaspoon	–	1 mL
	½ teaspoon	–	2 mL
	¾ teaspoon	–	4 mL
	1 teaspoon	–	5 mL
	1 tablespoon	–	15 mL
	¼ cup	–	59 mL
	⅓ cup	–	79 mL
	½ cup	–	118 mL
	⅔ cup	–	156 mL
	¾ cup	–	177 mL
	1 cup	–	235 mL
	2 cups or 1 pint	–	475 mL
	3 cups	–	700 mL
	4 cups or 1 quart	–	1 L
	½ gallon	–	2 L
	1 gallon	–	4 L

OVEN TEMPERATURES

FAHRENHEIT	CELSIUS (APPROXIMATE)
250°F	120°C
300°F	150°C
325°F	165°C
350°F	180°C
375°F	190°C
400°F	200°C
425°F	220°C
450°F	230°C

WEIGHT EQUIVALENTS

U.S. STANDARD	METRIC (APPROXIMATE)
½ ounce	15 g
1 ounce	30 g
2 ounces	60 g
4 ounces	115 g
8 ounces	225 g
12 ounces	340 g
16 ounces or 1 pound	455 g

INDEX

ACKNOWLEDGMENTS

Once again, I must thank my wonderfully patient and tenacious wife, Joan, who regularly inquired whether I was planning on writing today, tomorrow, or sometime soon. When I had procrastinated enough, she asked about the next deadline. And when it was imminent, she stepped in, whisking away anything that beeped, vibrated, or flashed. Without Joan, you would not be reading this book.

A big shout-out to our children, Alex, Cameron, and Lindsay, for their encouragement, support, and amusement as I periodically shared my ideas and progress with them.

Thanks also to my editor, Van Van Cleave from Callisto Media, whose positive attitude and feedback always made my writing better.

Finally, thanks to all you home cooks who picked up my first book, *Easy Chinese Cookbook: Restaurant Favorites Made Simple*. When you shared how much you enjoyed the recipes, posted a picture, or asked a question, you made my day.

ABOUT THE AUTHOR

Chris Toy has been teaching Asian cooking for over 30 years. Adopted by Alfred and Grace Toy, a Chinese-American couple, Chris arrived in the United States from Hong Kong in 1958. He graduated from Bowdoin College, then earned a master's degree in teaching from Brown University. Since then, he has worked as a teacher, principal, and international educational consultant. Chris learned Chinese cooking from his mother at home and in restaurant kitchens. Chris started teaching Chinese cooking on weekends at a local kitchen store in Portland, Maine. Today, he also teaches adult education classes in several communities around Bath, Maine, where he lives with his wife, Joan. His popular, hands-on classes are built around a deep appreciation for simply prepared food using fresh, local ingredients. A Registered Maine Guide, Chris also enjoys the woods and waters of Maine's great outdoors. Of course, preparing and sharing good food is always a highlight of his excursions. You can find him online at ChrisToy.net, and subscribe to his YouTube cooking channel at YouTube.com/user/cmtoy.

CPSIA information can be obtained
at www.ICGtesting.com
Printed in the USA
JSHW050219181021
19626JS00005B/5